Dancing Christmas Carols

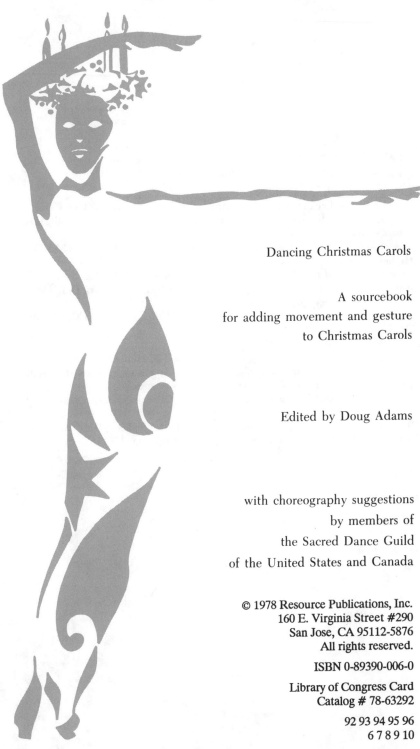

Dancing Christmas Carols

A sourcebook
for adding movement and gesture
to Christmas Carols

Edited by Doug Adams

with choreography suggestions
by members of
the Sacred Dance Guild
of the United States and Canada

© 1978 Resource Publications, Inc.
160 E. Virginia Street #290
San Jose, CA 95112-5876
All rights reserved.

ISBN 0-89390-006-0

Library of Congress Card
Catalog # 78-63292

92 93 94 95 96
6 7 8 9 10

Acknowledgements

Cover design and book design by George F. Collopy

Photos (right to left, top to bottom):

Inside cover — Dickins' Christmas Carol - Finale; "The Cherry Tree Carol"; shoulder isolation for "Peace" in "Glory Be To God In The Highest"/Huff, Jazz Gloria - Step E.

Page 6 — "Good Will," final position in chorus of "Glory Be To God In The Highest"/Huff.

Page 14 — Angel tells Mary the good news — from Chapter 10.

Page 21 — "Cherry Tree Carol" — Martin Overholt: tree; Mary Craighill: Mary; Louis Topler: Joseph.

Page 36 — Use of wreaths with children's choir at First Church UCC, Oberlin, OH.

Page 63 — Photo by J. Huff.

Page 77 — "Highest" in "Glory Be To God In The Highest"/Huff.

Page 130 — Dance Choir in Tacoma, WA, doing "Angels we have heard on high, sweetly singing o'er the plains"; and "Gloria in excelsis."

Page 133 — Dance Choir in Hanover, NH, doing "For poor onery people" in "I Wonder As I Wander."

Back cover — "News" from "Good Christian Folk, Rejoice"/Huff; Act V — Reprise of first Cratchit family scene from "A Christmas Carol."

table of Contents

oreward

Christmas is a most appropriate season for adding dance to the other art forms used in expressing the great joy of the season. Throughout history, more persons have been involved in dance at Christmas than at any other time. This is understandable since the very forms of Christmas carols encourage the full involvement of all persons. The word "carol" itself means to "dance with singing." Carols incorporate forms of dancing that in different periods of history have evoked enthusiastic and joyful participation by all.

Dancing Christmas Carols includes movement ideas for all persons to add to the joy and celebration of the holiday season. Many traditional and contemporary carols are presented in this volume, complete with choreographic descriptions. In chapters three through six, Carla DeSola, Peter Madden, Karen McClintock, Margaret Taylor, and Joan Huff share ways for people of all ages and abilities to move as they sing Christmas carols at home, at play, or in worship. Then in chapters seven through ten, Erika Thimey, Mary Craighaill, Virginia Shuker, and Margaret Taylor choreograph carols for soloists and dance choirs to skillfully transform the Word into flesh at Christmas.

Most carols are treated only once in this book. But, for a few carols, several different choreographies may be found here. Especially when a choir dances for others, it is good to present two or three different choreographies of the same carol to stimulate thought among the spectators. To present one dance invites people to contemplate whether they like or do not like to dance; but to present two or three different choreographies of the same carol invites people to consider which dance they find most helpful and why. Some people will prefer dances that stress vertical movement, and others will prefer dances that stress the horizontal. Some will prefer peaceful dances; and others will prefer energetic dances.

Beneath these preferences are a person's views of the world and of God, and of how God acts in the world. Criticisms of carol dances might be viewed as invitations to discuss theology and to stretch all of our concepts of God. Through this process we become aware of God acting in a wide variety of different circumstances from a dirty, smelly, noisy stable, all the way through an agonizing crucifixion, to the resurrection of the body and the birth of the Church amidst diverse expressions of the Word.

The widespread customs of caroling, of holiday get-togethers, of office Christmas parties, and other joyful gatherings during this season of wonder, are all appropriate situations in which the dimension of movement can be added to the celebration. The following pages tell you how to do it, explain the history of carol dances, and set forth some theological considerations that show how these joyful movements can be expressions of Christian faith. All you need to add is yourself, in both voice and body. Merry Christmas!

Doug Adams
Berkeley, CA
May, 1978

1 Dancing Carols: An Introduction To Dance In Worship

The joyful season of Christmas is much more than a religious feast in the world. It is celebrated by most Christians, regardless of denomination. It is also celebrated by some Jews, people of eastern religions, and, in some way, by millions of people who do not profess or participate in any organized religion.

The heightened feeling of joy present at this time of year calls forth expressions of many kinds: parties, gift giving, caroling, and a universal warmth. How natural to add movement and gesture expressions, especially when caroling!

There are several important dynamics to remember when dancing Christmas carols. First of all, dance steps should be demonstrated in a way that can be learned and executed by everyone. Too much attention to precise and graceful gestures excludes many people. At the same time, dance steps should be taken with as energetic a bounce or leap as possible. High energy in the dance form has its roots deep in western history. Medieval carols have this energetic form in common with first century Jewish and Christian sacred dance. For Jewish worship in the Temple courtyard, rejoicing with music was accompanied by acrobatic leaps in dances done by leading rabbis. Rejoicing and dancing were synonymous for first century Jews and for Christians who spoke Aramaic, the common tongue of Jesus' time. It is little wonder that Jesus is reported to have said things like, "Rejoice in that day, and leap for joy." (Luke 6:23)[1] If dance fails to generate joyfulness in the dancers, it may be because the form of the dance is too delicate and graceful, and some enthusiastic leaps are needed, especially when people sing words such as "joy" or "rejoice." Leaps have an advantage in that they may be done up in the air even by people who are standing in a crowd and are unable to move horizontally. Theologically, energetic leaps in sacred dance reassert that God is an active God, and that God made all parts of our bodies and not just the upper torso, arms, and head.

Another important point to remember is that dance steps to carols have usually been done in the larger forms of either circle dances or line dances, or both. As the following chapter shows, both of these forms develop a sense of community that transcends the dancers by having the dancers focus beyond themselves to God, the center of the circle in a circle dance, or the destination of the line in a line dance. In worship, although circle dances may be done at times to celebrate the body of Christ of which believers are a part, the march (the procession and recession) is the paradigmatic form for Christian sacred dance. The circle dance tends to stress God's immanence, while the line dance stresses God's transcendence. Both deserve a place in worship. But the most popular line dance in the history of Christian worship took the shape of a march (at processions and recessions). As a dance form, the march stresses historical development rather than cyclical ways in the world, and expresses a faith that God leads us, as well as that God is in our midst.

The most common processional or line dance was the tripudium step. Tripudium means "three step." It is done by taking three steps forward and one step back, three steps forward and one step back, and so forth. This step is easily done because it fits any 4/4 or 2/4 hymn. Tripudium came to be translated "jubilate" or "jubilation," a word often found in the chorus of hymns. The chorus of hymns is a natural place for the tripudium to appear. It is also a natural place for people to dance, for "chorus," like "carol," means "dance." The chorus is the repeated part of a hymn that everyone knows and to which everyone can most easily add movement. The "stanza" means "stand" or "halt" and is that changing part of a hymn which people do not so readily know, and so they stop singing to listen to this part sung by others. Years ago, the tripudium steps danced during the chorus were not done in single file, but rather were done in processions with many abreast with arms linked in row after row. These rows would move through the streets and into the Church and around it during the hymns of the service, and then out through the streets as a recessional. Moving three or four or more abreast makes the doing of this step much easier — one can hardly fall behind. Taking three steps forward and one back leads to an optimistic spirit that sees setback in the context of ongoing progress.[2] "Joy to the World," "Amen," and many other modern carols may be sung while doing this tripudium step. Both the sense of joy and the sense of Amen ("so be it") are forcefully expressed in this step and form.

Another important point is that the form of many carols with stanzas and choruses further encourages dance by allowing diversity of expression within the community. While all may join in simple movement to the chorus, a few highly skilled dancers may dance the stanzas with more elaborate choreography. By utilizing this form, the community need not reduce everyone to the lowest common denominator in its liturgical expressions, but may allow an enriching diversity as was envisioned by the apostle Paul.[3]

An example of such diversity is given in the following design for the carol

10

"We Three Kings." During the chorus, all may sing and as many as wish may join in dancing the tripudium (as described above) in rows of three or four persons abreast with arms linked. They may move down aisles or in wide circles in open areas. But on each stanza, all stop and watch a soloist or dance choir do movements that embody gold (for the first verse), frankincense (for the second verse), and myrrh (for the third verse). The dance for each stanza should avoid mimetic interpretation of each word or phrase and instead should dance forth the central dynamic of each verse. For instance, the verse concerning the gift of gold could incorporate dull cloddy movements that are transformed into refined regal ones. The gift of frankincense verse could move with the swirling motif of incense making its way among the people. The verse with the gift of myrrh could include gestures which touch and enfold many different individuals, just as myrrh was used to wrap and honor the dead. The solo dancer or dance choir members might most appropriately move arms linked with the others during the choruses and then detach themselves to dance the stanzas. At the end of each stanza, the dance soloist or dance choir members would rejoin the main procession for the chorus. In this way, those who dance the stanzas about the gifts carried by the wise men are themselves borne along with the procession. By having several persons dance the stanza in different places among the entire group, one overcomes problems of poor visibility at any one place while people are standing or moving. Also, by having several different dancers doing solos in different locations, one avoids the temptation of doing a dance where all members of the dance choir copy each other and perform uniform movements. Even if the dance choir members are moving together in one place, diverse enriching movements from each dancer should be encouraged. Such added complexity is the gift of dance choirs and witnesses to the nature of the body of Christ that Paul describes. We are of one body, but different parts bring different gifts.

The stress on energetic leaps and line dances advised earlier for congregational folk dance is also to be stressed for the forms of dance by soloists and dance choirs, although it should be stressed in more sophisticated ways. There is a tendency for dance choirs to do dances that are too pretty and too well rounded with low energy levels. The principles outlined in this chapter encourage dancers to do bolder dances with straight lines and not just circles. Often the cause of an insipid sacred dance is not just poor technique, but insipid theological and liturgical background.[4] If one has not read much of the Bible and has experienced only quiet, clean, and harmonius worship, one is likely to envision God as present only when all is quiet and harmonius and clean. As a result, one is likely to do sappy dances with slowly and harmoniously developed circular movements stressing the upper torso, hands, and head. But if one has read the Bible deeply and experienced life deeply and worshipped in a variety of different settings with different persons, one is likely to envision God as moving at times abruptly to disrupt the temple, to lay low the mighty, to shake the foundations. Dance may very well witness to the God that speaks in the stillness; but, if it is to be faithful to the biblical record, it must also witness to the God who speaks through mighty acts.

For the dance choir or the solo dancer, these theological concerns will be translated into the utilization of all parts of the body (for God created all parts and called them good) and not just the upper half of the body. The emphasis will be on locomotive movements instead of axial movement; i.e. the dance will move out into other spaces (line dance) and not center around a fixed point (circle dance). The emphasis will be on high energy expressed through sharp lines and not just on low energy expressed through harmonious circular movements. This means that angular, rather than circular patterns for the arms are to be developed. Of all seasons of the year, Christmas is the time for the boldest dances as witness to incarnation and creation. This is the one season when we may speak openly of a pregnant woman and we focus praise on a part of the body that at other times of the year is unmentioned, at least in worship. Christmas, let us have dances that affirm that we have pelvises and that God made them. The chapter on "Updating Christmas Carols to Jazz" suggests some possibilities along these lines drawn from Latin dance. Such dance is not new in Christian worship. In medieval Spanish Catholic Masses at certain times, the flamenco was the form of the dance, and such dance has been revived in some Spanish Masses. Pretending that we do not have pelvises in worship does not reduce eroticism but only heightens it by suggesting a dualism: i.e. that someone other than God created and rules part of the body. Putting pelvises in their proper place is accomplished by having them praise God.[5]

Our dances should acknowledge the brokenness and sin in the world, as is done with the backstep in the tripudium. We once did a danced prayer of confession to the song, "We Shall Overcome." We used a reverse tripudium step to witness to the sad decline of government programs and our own concerned dedication for the poor in the United States. In other words, we did the tripudium with one step forward and three steps backwards, one step forward and three steps backward. During confessional prayer, such an expression of brokenness is most appropriate. Such brokenness should usually be seen in the context of the ongoing word. We should remember, lest our dances become superficially joyful, that it is in brokenness on the cross that God acts to save the world, and that it is in the breaking of the bread that we are incorporated into the resurrected body. As a result of the glad birth in Bethlehem, many innocent children were slain by Herod. Grace and judgment come together in the Word and so should come together in the dance. The joyful dancing at

Christmas that this book details is possible because of the Word: the one who realizes all the persecutions we will face (Luke 6:22) and concludes (in Luke 6:23) "Rejoice in that day, and leap for joy."

Social events, as well as worship and educational events with Christmas carols should end with a going out to share Christmas carols with others. Sharing in circle dances and fine solo and choir dances in worship is appropriate to center and strengthen the body of Christ; but such entering is not an end in itself. Such dances should be included in the larger context of recessing into the world where the good news is shared. An afternoon or evening of caroling throughout the community (downtown, in retirement homes, jails, or hospitals, etc.) can immediately follow any celebration incorporating these Christmas carols. Sharing the good news is a result not only of what we bring with us from our faith, but also what we discover in the world, for Christ is more than we have realized and is moving beyond the confines of the Church. We must be moving out if we would greet and follow Christ.

Doug Adams is president of the International Sacred Dance Guild. He teaches "worship and the arts" at the Pacific School of Religion, and serves on the doctoral faculty in "Theology and the Arts" at the Graduate Theological Union, Berkeley, California. He is a fellow in the North American Academy of Liturgy and serves on the editorial board of *Modern Liturgy*. His publications in the field of dance include the books *Congregational Dancing In Christian Worship* and *Involving The People In Dancing Worship: Historic and Contemporary Forms*. He is ordained and has served as pastor in churches in California and Washington.

1. For a history of early Jewish and Christian dance in worship, refer to Adams' *Congregational Dancing In Christian Worship* (Austin: Sharing Company, 1977).
2. Cf. Adams' "Triumph and Tripudium: A Gesture of Jubilation To Avoid Passing Over The Joy of Holy Thursday," *Modern Liturgy*, Vol. 5 No. 2 (March, 1978), p. 8.
3. Cf. I Corinthians 12 and Adams' "Celebrating Our Unity and Diversity In Liturgical Dance," *Modern Liturgy*, Vol. 4 No. 3, (March, 1977), pp. 4-5.
4. Cf. Judith Rock's new book *Theology In The Shape Of The Dance: Dance In Worship And Theological Process* (Austin: Sharing Company, 1978) for many implications of theology for dance and dance for theology. Particularly for dance solos and dance choirs, we need her criteria for sacred dance to be good it must first of all be good dance. She is also helpful in noting that some sacred dance solos and dance choir pieces need not be fully seen by all in the congregation: i.e. there is a place for mystery in faith and worship and sacred dance.
5. In his book *Congregational Dancing In Christian Worship*, Doug Adams showed conclusively that dance was eliminated from the Catholic Church in the late medieval period not because it was erotic, but because it led to an equality between priest and bishop and people in an era when the hierarchy was striving to distinguish itself from the people. Cf. *Congregational Dancing In Christian Worship*, op. cit., chapter 2.

Dancing Carols: Historical Beginnings

During the first twelve centuries, Christian religious dance consisted mainly of variations on the carol, which is a song-with-dance form. These were ring-dances and line-dances and were especially appropriate for liturgical use because their emphasis was on the communal aspect of the dancing group. The focus of the circle dance was on the center of the circle, on what was believed or celebrated. The focus of the line carol was on the destination of the dancers; not on themselves, but on something outside themselves: God. In addition, the carol was an impersonal form of dance as far as the sexes were concerned. Both the line and circle dances could be danced by groups of men, groups of women, or by any combination of the two. The emphasis was not on the possible relationships between individual dancers, but on their relationship as a group and their common reason for dancing.

The carol is a song-with-dance form. As such, it combines a nonobjective carol lyric with an objective, impersonal carol dance form. The words of the carol are nonobjective in that they nearly always appeal to the emotions of the hearers. The nativity carols, for example, do not simply narrate the events of Jesus' birth as an objective ballad would. Instead, they tell the story of the birth through its emotional and spiritual effect on other people. One French carol which begins, "Neighbor, what was that sound, I pray," describes a village awakened at night by the Baby's cries. The villagers in the course of the lyrics decide what gifts to give Him. Included in their list are someone's carpenter tools and someone else's pan of new milk. The dance form which accompanied the carol lyrics, however, was objective: a circle or line of people moving in unison. This combination of emotional, moving lyrics, and the communal, impersonal dance form can be seen as an appropriate folk art response to the message of the Incarnation. Individuals are personally moved by the news of God-with-us in the world, and they respond by becoming part of the Body of Christ.

Centuries ago, carols were sung and danced in stanza-chorus form. For the stanza, the group stood still while the leader sang in the center of the ring or at the head of the line. For the chorus, the group "chorused" or functioned as a chorus with everyone singing and dancing together. The chief characteristic of the carol lyric is the presence of the chorus or refrain. The medieval term for the refrain of the carol was *burden*. The

15

use of this term *(burden)* for the refrain of the carol may be related to the nature of the carol as an artistic response to the Incarnation.

The origin of this term *burden* is uncertain. *The Oxford Dictionary* states that it represents a confusion of the words *bourdon, burden,* and *burthen. Bourdon* is defined as a drone, as in an instrument or in the lowest voice of a medieval song. This word became completely confused with *burden/burthen* which seems (among other relations and meanings) to be related to birth, as the child in the womb, called a *burden.* The *th* and *d* were used interchangeably.

A Hebrew word, *massa,* is also translated as *burden* in the Old Testament, with the sense of lifting up the voice to proclaim the word of the Lord. A refrain which caught up the gist of meaning of a poem also was called a burden, somewhat out of confusion with *bourdon* as a musical term.

Bourdon also meant a pilgrim's staff, derived from the Latin *burdo,* or donkey. This form of bourdon presents interesting possibilities in terms of the origin of the technical term *burden* for the carol refrain. During the time of the medieval pilgrimages, pilgrims on their way home would often gather in the streets of towns where they would sing songs which they had composed on their journeys. The songs would be about the life of a pilgrim, about various miracles and martyrdoms, about places seen on their journeys and about the life of Christ. Like modern streetsingers, they hoped for money from the passers by in return for their efforts. Menestrier, a seventeenth century French Jesuit dance historian, describes them, "singing with their staves (bourdons) in their hands, and their hats and mantles fantastically adorned with shells, and emblems painted in various colors..."[1]

The *Historical Anthology of Music* contains the following fourteenth century Italian lyric by Giovanni Da Florentia:

Io Son Un Pellegrin
(I Am A Pilgrim)

Burden: I am a pilgrim who goes seeking alms,
Crying mercy for God's sake.

Verse: And I go singing with fine voice,
With sweet appearance and blond tresses.

Burden: I am a pilgrim who goes seeking alms,
Crying mercy for God's sake.

16

Verse: I have nothing but the *pilgrim's stave* and wallet,
            And I cry out and cry out
            and there is no one who answers.

Burden: I am a pilgrim who goes seeking alms,
            Crying mercy for God's sake.

Verse: And when I am hoping for fair weather,
            A contrary wind arises against me.

Burden: I am a pilgrim who goes seeking alms,
            Crying mercy for God's sake. (HAM #51)

It could be that the idea of the staff which supported the pilgrim, the burden-bearing donkey, and the drone which supported the musical structure of a multi-voice song became associated with the refrain of the carol, during which the group of singers and dancers responded to and supported the leader.

The term *burden* might also be related to the occurence of the Middle English word *burde* in several carols. Again, *The Oxford Dictionary* says that the meaning here is uncertain. The early carol, *Alma Redemptoris Mater*, contains the following verses:

Verse 1:   "As I lay upon a night,
               my thought was upon a *burde*
               so bright,
               that men clepen Mary, full of might,
               Alma redemptoris mater.

Verse 2:   Jesu that sittest in heavn light
               Grant us comen before thy sight
               With that *burde* that is so bright,
               Alma redemptoris mater."
               (*Medieval Carols* #4)

The burden of the carol is "Alma redemptoris mater," which means "Mother of the soul's redeemer." Mary, who is "Alma redemptoris mater" is also called *burde*. In a later German carol (fifteenth century), called *Joseph Lieber* (Joseph Dearest), Jesus is called "bird."

"Thou my lazy heart has stirred,
Thou the Father's eternal word,
Greater than naught that ear hath heard,
Thou tiny *bird* of love,
Thou son of Mary."

(The Oxford Book of Carols)

Among the meanings suggested for *burde* are "bride" and "bird." It is possible that *burde* may have some relation to burden. In any case, all these words are rich in associations to the meaning of Incarnation, which was a typical subject of medieval carols:

> *Burthen* in the sense of the child in the womb and therefore suggesting the Nativity;
> *Burden* as a translation of the Hebrew *massa* or proclaiming the word of the Lord;
> *Burde* used for both a young woman and a child;
> *Bourdon* as the supporting voice in a part-song;
> and *Burdon*, or pilgrim's staff.

The carol refrain, or burden, generally stated succinctly what was being sung or danced about; in other words, the refrain contained the most important part, the burden, of the carol's message.

But even as the carol was developing and acquiring its constellation of meanings and associations, the carol dance began to be replaced by the couple dance. The couple dance developed as a result of the code of chivalry, or courtly love, which was a prominent social and literary phenomenon of the twelfth century. Chivalry affected both secular and liturgical dance forms. Socially, the couple dance began to replace the communal dance. Although the couples were usually arranged in a line or ring, the focus of the dance was on the possible relationships which might develop within the couples. The focus began to shift away from the communal reason for dancing. The focus of the circle dance shifted from the center of the circle to its periphery.

The couple dance presented anew the problematic possibility of the religious dance becoming dance for a primarily humanistic purpose. In the thirteenth and fourteenth centuries, some developments in religious music led to what one author described as "the trend toward the production of music for music's sake — a move in opposition to the long-held philosophy of the church."[2] The danger of inappropriateness in liturgical dance sets in whenever the focus shifts from the function of the dance to the personalities of the dancers so that they become the end purpose of the dance.

Religious dance began to be threatened by the same tendency toward "art for art's sake." During the period of the development of the carol dance, the Christian liturgy had objectivity as one of its major characteristics. The point of Gregorian chant was not to move the worshipper emotionally, not to focus him inside himself, but to proclaim the Word, to focus him outside himself on God. It may be that this long tradition of objectivity in the liturgy accounts for the tremendous medieval creativity in religious architecture, manuscript illumination, drama, and music. This objectivity was characteristic of the dance element of the carol form. Creativity frequently seems to take place when two distinctions meet; inner and outer, male and female, form and content, emotional and objective. The carol form combined the objective dance form with an emotional personal lyric form. These two elements, personality and objectivity, embodied the human response to the Incarnation. In the face of the rising tide of Renaissance humanism, preserving the objectivity of both liturgy and dance was a concern of many medieval church leaders. This led to an increasing demand that the focus of the Mass be on God rather than on individual human beings and their feelings. At this point, as the more humanistic couple dance replaced the carol, religious dance began to move outside the sanctuary, into the churchyard, and onto the pageant wagon. It remained here through the Renaissance period and the period of reformation which followed.

1. Edmonstoune Duncan, *The Story of the Carol*, p. 30. (While Duncan is not always a reliable source, he has faithfully translated into English short sections of *Des Ballets Anciens et Modernes* by Jesuit Claude Francois Menestrier, a pioneer study on the ballet that is still available only in the French edition published originally in 1682 by Guignard of Paris.)

2. William Rice, *A Concise History of Church Music*, p. 25.

A good survey of the history of religious dance is presented in *A Time To Dance* by Margaret Fisk Taylor (Austin: The Sharing Company, 1967).

Judith Rock teaches "dance in worship" at Pacific School of Religion in the Graduate Theological Union, Berkeley, California. She is an ordained minister in the Presbyterian tradition having received the M. Div.; and she received the M.A. from Mills College with a thesis on the Jesuit use of ballet in the seventeenth century. She serves on the Board of Directors of the International Sacred Dance Guild. She is the author of the recently published volume *Theology In The Shape of Dance: Dance In Worship and Theological Process*. She performs solo dances as well as creates choreographies for dance groups. She has organized continuing dance choirs and recently delivered the prestigious McCall lectures in Berkeley through the medium of dance as well as the spoken word.

part one

Carols For Just About Everyone

3 Folk Dancing Christmas Carols

The two things I like most about working with carols is that they are very lively and very flexible. Their quick tempo helps to create an atmosphere of excitement and joy for those who sing, dance, or watch. They are flexible because the chorus and stanza arrangement is ideal for solo and chorus dances, and all of the dances choreographed here can be used for eight to twenty skilled or unskilled dancers of all ages. Elaborations may be added for more skilled dancers to accompany the group.

GOD REST YE MERRY GENTLEFOLK
18th Century English Carol

Choreography by Patty Simpson-Stanton, Roger Wedell, and Pat Dougherty

God rest ye merry gentlefolk,
Let nothing you dismay,
For Jesus Christ our Savior
Was born upon this day,

In one large circle, facing inward, holding hands...and moving to the right, with a hora step, begin on the word "rest" and step to the side on your right foot, cross the left foot behind, step to the right on the right foot again and kick the left foot across in front, then step on it, and kick the right foot across in front. Repeat three times to the right.

To save us all from Satan's power
When we were gone astray.

Running steps to the right.

Chorus:
O tidings of comfort and joy,
comfort and joy,

All move into the center, arms closing around each other's waists.

O tidings of comfort and joy.

Open out into the larger circle again.

From God, our heavenly Maker,
A blessed angel came;
And unto certain shepherds
Brought tidings of the same:

How that in Bethlehem was born
The Son of God by name.

Chorus

"Fear not, then," said the angel,
"Let nothing you affright;
This day is born a Savior,
Of a pure virgin bright,

To free all those who trust in him
From Satan's power and might."

Chorus

Now to the Lord sing praises,
All you within this place,
And with true love and unity
Each other now embrace;

This holy tide of Christmas
Doth bring redeeming grace.

Chorus

ANGELS WE HAVE HEARD ON HIGH
Traditional French Carol
Choreography by Patty Simpson-Stanton, Roger Wedell, and Pat Dougherty

Angels we have heard on high,
Sweetly singing o'er the plains,

With everyone gathered in a circle, holding hands, begin walking to the right.

And the mountains in reply,
Echoing their joyous strains.

Now walk left on the second phrase.

Chorus:
Glo...........ri-a

Everyone raises hands high, and moves to the center and back out, two times in, two times out. (Four steps in, four steps out, repeat.)

In excelsis Deo

Experienced groups can do the grapevine here to the right, quickly. This goes: Step to the right with the right foot, cross the left foot behind, step on the right foot again, and cross the left leg in front. Repeat two times.

Others may wish to skip in a circle with arms lifted. (One small circle around to the right.)

Glo..........ri-a

Same as above, moving in and out.

In excelsis Deo

Same as above, to the left this time.

Shepherds, why this jubilee?
Why your joyous strains prolong?

Say what may the tidings be,
Which inspire your heavenly song.

Chorus

Come to Bethlehem and see
Him whose birth the angels sing;

Come adore on bended knee,
Christ, the Lord, the newborn King.

Chorus

O COME, O COME, EMMANUEL
Latin, 12th Century
Choreography by Karen Campbell McClintock

O come, O come, Emmanuel

And ransom captive Israel,

That mourns in lonely exile here

Until the Son of God appear.

This dance requires two circles, of equal numbers of people one inside the other. The inside group travels counter-clockwise, and the outer group clockwise. In the circles, walk slowly. Right hands are held up with bent elbows and touch as the two circles pass each other. Hands are held together only long enough to greet, and the motion continues.

Chorus:
Rejoice!

Rejoice!

The outer circle turns in toward the inner circle and the inner circle turns outward so each person ends up facing a partner. On the first "rejoice," right palms meet at waist level and are raised high. Repeat with left hands on second "rejoice."

Emmanuel, shall come to thee
O Israel!

Partners join both hands and slowly circle a full circle walking to the right.

O come, thou Dayspring, come and cheer
Our spirits by thine advent here;
Disperse the gloomy clouds of night,
And death's dark shadows put to flight.

Chorus

O come, thou Wisdom from on high,
And order all things, far and nigh;
To us the path of knowledge show,
And cause us in her ways to go.

Chorus

O come, Desire of nations, bind
All peoples in one heart and mind;
Bid envy, strife and quarrels cease;
Fill the whole world with heaven's peace.

GOOD CHRISTIAN FOLK REJOICE
German-Latin Carol, 14th Century
Choreography by Karen Campbell McClintock

Good Christian folk, rejoice

This dance begins in a circle with everyone facing inward, arms at sides. Step to the right on the right foot, and brush the left foot across in front, hopping on the right at the same time. Repeat to the left (it goes step, brush-hop, and again step, brush-hop).

With heart and soul and voice;

Repeat as above.

Give ye heed to what we say:
Jesus Christ is born today.

Everyone skips to the center.
Everyone skips backward, out again.

Ox and ass before him bow,
And he is in the manager now.

Hands are folded across chests, and everyone bows slowly down to a kneeling position.

Christ is born today,

Right leg lifts so that the right foot rests on the floor. The body lifts up (with the arms uncrossing and reaching upward) to a standing position.

Christ is born today.

With arms still open, but lifted high, turn to the right. This can be walked, or the right leg can serve as a pivot point for a turn.

Good Christian folk, rejoice
With heart and soul and voice;

Now ye hear of endless bliss;
Jesus Christ was born for this!

He hath opened the heavenly door,
And man is blessed evermore.

Christ was born for this!

Christ was born for this!

Rather than bowing this time, lift the arms, palms up, straight out in front, then higher so that on "blessed" elbows bend and each person's palm touches the top of his/her head. Arms lower, and people turn as above.

27

Good Christian folk, rejoice,
With heart and soul and voice;

Now ye need not fear the grave;
Jesus Christ was born to save!

Calls you one and calls you all,
To gain his ever lasting hall.

Christ was born to save!

Christ was born to save!

Everyone joins hands, and moves into the circle, wrapping arms about one another. In the center arch and look skyward, then return to the larger circle to finish with the turn described above.

GOOD KING WENCESLAS
Traditional English Carol
Choreography by Karen Campbell McClintock

Good King Wenceslas look'd out,
On the Feast of Stephen,

When the snow lay round about,
Deep and crisp and even:

Brightly shone the moon that night,
Tho' the frost was cruel,

This begins in follow-the-leader style. It is a broken circle, with hands held; and a person chosen to be King Wenceslas is the leader. Everyone steps lively as they wind about the room. The step goes: step on the right foot, and bend the right knee. The left foot is lifted off the ground as the right knee bends. The rhythm goes step, bend, step, bend, etc.

When a poor man came in sight,
Gathering winter fuel.

A person who is designated to be the poor man, steps out of the chain.

'Hither, page, and stand by me,
If thou know'st it, telling,
Yonder peasant, who is he?
Where and what his dwelling?'

'Sire, he lives a good league hence,
Underneath the mountain,
Right against the forest fence,
By Saint Agnes' fountain.'

The last person in the chain (the page) comes forward and links elbows with the leader to chat. The chain of "step-bend" continues.
(The poor man pretends to gather wood during this time.)

"Bring me flesh, and bring me wine,
Bring me pine logs hither:
Thou and I will see him dine,
When we bear them thither."

Dancers continue in a chain as the carol continues.

Page and monarch, forth they went,
Forth they went together;
Through the rude wind's wild lament
And the bitter weather.

"Sire, the night is darker now,
And the wind blows stronger;
Fails my heart, I know not how;
I can go no longer."

"Mark my footsteps, my good page;
Tread thou in them boldly:
Thou shalt find the winter's rage
Freeze thy blood less coldly."

The leader of the group forms the group into a circle again, and steps big bold steps (as if in snow); others follow behind. The circle encloses the poor man.

In his master's steps he trod,
Where the snow lay dinted;
Heat was in the very sod
Which the Saint had printed.

Therefore Christians, now be sure,
Wealth or rank possessing,
Ye who now will bless the poor,
Shall yourselves find blessing.

The circle closes into the middle and people touch (as in blessing) the poor man; he joins the circle at the end and everyone stands arm in arm.

WHILE BY MY SHEEP
17th Century Hymn
Choreography by Karen Campbell McClintock

While by my sheep
I watched at night,
Glad tidings brought
An angel bright:

Two circles are formed, the inside circle going clockwise, and the outside circle going counter-clockwise. The step is the traditional tripudium step (three steps forward and one step back). Hands are linked with the left hand reaching back over shoulder, and the right hand forward into the left hand of the person in front of you.

Chorus:
How great my joy

Everyone drops hands and turns to the other circle at this time. The inside group turns to face the outside group, and vice-versa. With arms folded across chests, each person in the outside group skips in his/her own small circle one complete turn.

Great my joy

Each person on the inside skips in his/her own circle with hands folded across chests.

Joy, joy, joy!	Outside circle turns in the same manner as above, with arms raised and reaching upward this time.
Joy, joy, joy!	Inside circle repeats what outside group just did.
Praise we the Lord in heav'n on high	Outside group joins hands and slowly lifts them.
Praise we the Lord in heav'n on high.	Inside group also joins hands and slowly lifts them.

There shall be born,
so he did say,
In Bethlehem
a Child today.

Chorus

There shall He lie,
in manger mean,
Who shall redeem the world from sin.

Chorus

Lord, evermore to me be nigh,
Then shall my heart be filled with joy!

HERE WE COME A-WASSAILING
19th Century
Choreography by Karen-Campbell McClintock

Here we come a-wassailing
Among the leaves so green,
It's here we come a wand'ring
So fair to be seen:

Chorus:

Love and joy come to you,
And to you your wassail too,

And God bless you, and send you
A Happy New Year.

Our wassail cup is made
Of the rosemary tree,
And so is your beer
Of the best barley:

Chorus

We are not daily beggars
That beg from door to door,
But we are neighbours' children
Whom you have seen before:

Chorus

Good Master and good Mistress,
As you sit by the fire,
Pray think of us poor children
Who are wandering in the mire:

Chorus

We have a little purse
Made of ratching leather skin;
We want some of your small change
To line it well within:

Chorus

Call up the Butler of this house,
Put on his golden ring;
Let him bring us a glass of beer,
And the better we shall sing:

Chorus

Bring us out a table,
And spread it with a cloth;
Bring us out some mouldy cheese,
And some of your Christmas loaf:

In a circle, skip eight counts, counterclockwise. Repeat going clockwise.

Walk counter-clockwise in a little step, bend, step, bend movement.

Everyone joins hands and moves into the center then out.
Repeat into and out of the circle.

32

Chorus

God bless the Master of this house,
Likewise the Mistress too;
And all the little children
That round the table go:

Chorus

And all your kind and kinsfolk
That dwell both far and near;
I wish you a Merry Christmas,
And a happy New Year.

Chorus

LORD OF THE DANCE
Text by Sydney Carter
Choreography by Dick Cohelan

1. I danced in the morning
when the world was begun,
and I danced in the moon
and the stars and the sun,
and I came down from heaven
and I danced on the earth
at Bethlehem I had my birth.

Everyone joins left hands in middle of circle (arms slightly raised).
Shuffle to the right.
At words "came down" drop arms and stomp the ground.

Chorus:

Dance then wherever you may be,
I am the Lord of the Dance said He,
and I'll lead you all
wherever you may be,
and I'll lead you all
in the dance said he.

Join hands in a circle. One person (e.g. with blue top) leads and everyone else follows. Try to maintain hand contact and move to the right. Highly spirited!

2. I danced for the scribe
and the pharisee
but they would not dance
and they wouldn't follow me.

Hands joined. Heads back haughtily. Barely shuffle to the right. Grimly.

I danced for the fishermen
for James and John.
They came with me
and the dance went on.

Drop hands. Throw hands (palms up) into the middle of circle (as if throwing a fishing net). Happily.

Chorus

Rejoin hands. Another person leads...

3. I danced on the Sabbath
and I cured the lame.
The holy people said
it was a shame.

Hop on one foot slowly to the right (as if lame).

They whipped and they stripped
and they hung me high
and they left me there
on a Cross to die.

Then at the words "whipped and stripped" release hands, put arms out straight to your sides and head back (as on a cross). Remain stationary or turn around very slowly.

Chorus

Rejoin hands. Next persons lead...

4. *I danced on a Friday*
when the sky turned black.
It's hard to dance
with the devil on your back.
They buried my body
and they thought I'd gone.
But I am the dance
and I still go on.

Walk to the right with head bowed
progressively lower and lower...

At "buried my body" be down on the
ground. Alone. No hand contact.

Chorus

Rejoin hands. Next person leads...

5. *They cut me down*
and I leapt up high.
I am the life
That'll never, never die.
I'll live in you
if you'll live in me
I am the Lord
of the dance said He.

Jump up and down, reaching up.
Move to the right.

Chorus

Rejoin hands. Next person leads.

Karen Campbell McClintock is serving as Associate Pastor at the First United Methodist Church in Santa Rosa, California. She is actively involved in a ministry of the arts, directing plays and leading dance workshops in Northern California. Her dance training includes many years of ballet and jazz and recent concentration in modern dance. She studied sacred dance with Carla DeSola in New York and at Pacific School of Religion. Having taught courses at Pacific School of Religion on "Dance As Prayer," she leads special dance workshops for women, youth, and seniors.

4 Dancing Carols With Children

With young children, the teacher or leader should rely on spontaneous movements and avoid prescribed patterns of movement for feet and arms. The following dances for Christmas carols with children provide suggestions for overall patterns within which children should be encouraged to express their creativity. It is a good idea to have the children listen to and sing the carol at least once before attempting to dance.

ANGELS WE HAVE HEARD ON HIGH

The beautiful carol "Angels We Have Heard On High," with its chorus of "Gloria in excelsis Deo," invites one to whirl around with a feeling of glory. The spiraling notes offer the child a musical pattern that he or she can express in spiraling turns. As they turn, they should learn to be aware of where they are in relation to others so that they fill the space freely, but without colliding with one another.

As they sing "Gloria," some of the children may want to turn three times which is the general division of the musical phrasing; some may wish to drift and turn; others may feel like turning more than three times because they enjoy turning. Encourage them to express themselves in whatever ways they find meaningful. Encourage the children to look up and around them as they turn.

At the close of the chorus, during the singing of "in excelsis Deo," there may be a turning or coming toward a center. Praying hands may be lifted during "in excelsis" (in the highest) and lowered to a position of prayer during "Deo." Sometimes the children like to kneel at this point or at the end.

Here are some general suggestions for the first and third stanzas.

Angels we have heard on high	The children gather from various parts of the room.
Sweetly singing o'er the plains,	They improvise with floating turns and arms extended.

And the mountains in reply	Everyone raises one arm and looks up, possibly moving away from the center.
Echo back their joyous strains.	A design similar to the one for line two is used, possibly in the opposite direction.

Chorus:
Gloria in excelsis Deo,
Gloria in excelsis Deo.

Shepherds, why this jubilee?
Why your joyous strain prolong?
Say what may the tidings be,
Which inspire your heavenly song.

Chorus

Come to Bethlehem and see	The children move toward the imaginary creche in the center.
Him of whom the angels sing	They swirl out from the center, extending an arm, as if inviting others to come to adore.
Come, adore on bended knee	Everyone comes to the center and kneels with head bowed.
Christ, our Lord, our newborn King	The arms may be lifted, widened, and brought to rest at sides, slightly extended, all with a sense of wonder.

Chorus

As the children sing "Gloria," they may think of the uplifted "O" of their arms made wide and high. Then their arms break apart at the top as though the children are catching a glimpse of more glory. The arm movement of forming a high arch and of spreading apart are linked with spiral turns.

38

The children will need to practice kneeling so that they will have grace and control. If the forward foot is turned out, there is more of a base; if the foot in the rear keeps the ball of the foot on the floor, there is more control and more ease in rising quickly. When the children kneel, they should not crouch down low unless there is some special reason to do so. Most of the time a straight kneel means that there could be a straight line from the knee that touches the ground up that thigh, up through the torso to the head. They should practice kneeling on each knee so that they can kneel equally well on either knee. When they are portraying this carol and come to a place where they wish to kneel, they should feel free to kneel on whichever knee they choose.

O LITTLE TOWN OF BETHLEHEM

For dancing this Christmas carol, each child may be supplied with a large cardboard star, six inches or larger in diameter. The star should have a loop of thread attached through a small hole pierced in one of the points of the star, so that the child is able to hang the star from his or her finger as he or she moves. The purpose of the stars is twofold. They serve as a springboard for this interpretation of the carol; but most important- ly, holding a star helps a child be less self-conscious. The child becomes absorbed in what he or she holds, and how the star moves, and is thus able to forget himself or herself.

The lead into creation of the dance could go something like: "We've been making stars for Christmas decorations. Let's be stars ourselves. Let's be like the stars that shone on that first Christmas when Jesus was born. We all know the carol "O Little Town of Bethlehem." Let's sing it and think of stars as we sing. Whenever we sing stars, let's raise our hands for a moment but keep right on singing." If the children do not know the first two stanzas of "O Little Town of Bethlehem," the words could be printed clearly on a blackboard or on a large sheet of paper propped up on an easel, wherever the children can read them easily. The children then sing the carol.

O little town of Bethlehem,
How still we see thee lie;
Above thy deep and dreamless sleep
The silent stars go by.
Yet in thy dark streets shineth
The everlasting Light;
The hopes and fears of all the years
Are met in thee tonight.

For Christ is born of Mary,
And gathered all above,
While mortals sleep,
The angels keep
Their watch of wondering love.
O morning stars, together
Proclaim the holy birth!
And praises sing to God the King,
And peace to all on earth!

How silently, how silently,
The wondrous gift is given!
So God imparts to human hearts
The blessings of his heaven.
No ear may hear his coming,
But in this world of sin,
Where meek souls will receive him,
still
The dear Christ enters in.

O holy Child of Bethlehem!
Descend to us, we pray;
Cast our our sin and enter in;
Be born in us today.
We hear the Christmas angels
The great glad tidings tell;
O come to us, abide with us,
Our Lord Emmanuel!

The leader may then ask the children what they should do if they are to
be like the stars in the carol; and the leader should indicate that they
need lots of ideas from everyone. The following ideas were expressed in
one group:

Karen: I can wrap my baby doll in a blanket and lay it on this low table.
Kevin: What does that have to do with stars?
Karen: That's the baby Jesus for the stars to shine on.
John: Let's use the stars we have been making. We can take the stars far
off first, and then start moving very slowly and quietly toward
Bethlehem.
Janet: I think we could kneel down and hold our stars up for the baby to
look at when we get close. Then we can move away and let someone else
have a turn.
John: When we sing "and gathered all above," we should all be together
then.

40

Kevin: I don't think we need to be together until we sing, "O morning stars, together/Proclaim the holy birth," Then we can all be together and hold our stars up high.

Leader: Why don't we try out some of these ideas? Then we can see just when we feel we should gather together.

Karen: I'll put my sweater here, to make a bed for the baby Jesus.

John: Come on over to this corner so we'll have a long way to come.

Kevin: Why don't we use two corners?

Karen: Does "proclaim" mean announce?

Janet: Yes, it means something like a news broadcast.

John: We can hold our stars up high to broadcast the news that Jesus is born.

Karen: And we can lower them when we sing, "And peace to all on earth!"

Kevin: Let's hum instead of singing while we go back to our corners.

Leader: These are all splendid ideas! Let's put them all together now. First we find our star homes and start out. We'll come in slowly, perhaps kneel by the baby, and move on until we come together and lift our stars high as we sing: "O morning stars together, Proclaim the holy birth!" We lower them as we sing, "And peace to all on earth." Then we hum softly as we return to our star homes.

The children then sing the carol enacting it as suggested from the discussion.

Then after the dancing, there is a brief discussion such as the following:

Leader: That is beautiful! Let's sit down together for a few minutes and tell what we liked best.

Janet: I liked coming in. I felt as if something surprising was happening. I liked kneeling for a minute too.

Kevin: I like turning like a planet when we were going back to our star homes. I don't like to think of words, so I liked the humming part.

John: I liked lifting my star up high, and I had mine higher than any of the others!

Karen: I think we should have Mary taking care of the baby. May I be Mary if we do it again?

Leader: We will do this again; if not right now, then when we meet next week. Perhaps then you'll have even more ideas for dancing and singing this carol.

THE TWELVE DAYS OF CHRISTMAS

This early carol was probably sung in the church or its courtyard to remind the people of the twelve days between the Christ Mass of the Nativity and Epiphany. When this carol became a secular folk carol sung and danced in circles in the market place, many of the words were too difficult to be remembered; so, many substitutes were made as the years went by. We can only make conjectures now. "A partridge in a pear tree" could have been a reference to "The Perfect Paraclete." The original meaning of this word is "mediator" or "intercessor." In I John 2:1, where Christ's role as advocate before God is mentioned, we have the appropriate meaning of "Paraclete." Surely this could be the first gift for the first day of Christmas. Christ on the cross (the tree) is a meaningful linking of Christmas and Easter.

"Two turtle doves" are mentioned as gifts in Luke 2:24 when the baby Jesus was brought to the temple around the eighth day. Of course "gold" is mentioned as a gift of the wise man. All of the other gifts mentioned are a hodgepodge of folk matters, but the carol was kept alive in its own way. And we keep it alive today. (In Hawaii, there are twelve Hawaiian gifts sung at Christmas time!)

I squeeze the ideas into words to give a few clues of how children may dance the carol. Twelve persons stand in a circle, each with a wreath in the right hand but each touching the adjacent person's wreath. They hold wreaths at shoulder height. They number off one through twelve. Most of the movements are done by all in unison unless otherwise indicated:

On the first day of Christmas
My true love gave to me

All take one step sideways to the right with the right foot, and close the side step with the left foot. While holding wreaths, raise hands overhead. All look up. Put right foot forward into the circle, and lower wreaths so that they are arms length to the front at shoulder level. All step back. These actions are repeated at the beginning of each stanza.

A partridge in a pear tree

No. 1 steps forward into circle, swings right hand forward and up, holding wreath. No. 1 returns to original position.

On the second day of Christmas
My true love gave to me

The group actions are repeated as in first stanza.

Two turtle doves *And a partridge in a pear tree*	No. 2 steps forward into circle, swings wreath forward and up and returns to original position. No. 1 holds wreath directly over and high above his or her head and turns in place once around taking tiptoe steps right in place while turning.
On the third day of Christmas *My true love gave to me*	The group actions are repeated.
Three French hens *Two turtle doves* *And a partridge in a pear tree*	No. 3 steps forward, etc. No. 2 turns in place with wreath held high. No. 1 (the same).
On the fourth day of Christmas *My true love gave to me*	The group actions are repeated.
Four calling birds *Three French hens* *Two turtle doves* *And a partridge in a pear tree*	No. 4 steps forward, etc. No. 3 turns in place, etc. No. 2 (the same). No. 1 (the same).
On the fifth day of Christmas *My true love gave to me* *Five gold rings*	The group actions are repeated. No. 5 is the only one who always does a longer design because this musical phrase is always sustained longer. No. 5 steps forward with wreath swung high on "five," then pulls wreath diagonally down and to left shoulder high on "gold"; then straight across to right shoulder high.
Four calling birds *Three French hens* *Two turtle doves* *And a partridge in a pear tree*	The rest continue their successive turning in place. And the whole dance pattern continues all the way up to twelve days of Christmas. Each time the carol reaches No. 5 (gold rings), that dancer may do a different variation: making a sign of the cross with the wreath moving up and from left to right or moving in and out of the circle in a whirling motion.

On the twelfth day of Christmas
My true love gave to me
Twelve pipers piping
Eleven lords a leaping
Ten drummers drumming
Nine ladies dancing
Eight maids a milking
Seven swams a swimming
Six geese a laying
Five gold rings
Four calling birds
Three French hens
Two turtle doves
And a partridge in a pear tree

Often as a closing, all will sing and lift their wreaths as they repeat "And a partridge in a pear tree" to give a unison ending.

O HOLY NIGHT

O, Holy night,
The stars are brightly shining,
It is the night of the dear Savior's birth.
Long lay the world
In sin and error pining,
Till He appeared and the spirit felt its worth.
A thrill of hope the weary world rejoices,
For yonder breaks
A new and glorious morn.
Fall on your knees!
Oh, hear the angel voices!
O night divine,
O night when Christ was born;
O night divine! O night, O night divine!

The French carol "O Holy Night" could serve well for a processional of worshippers. The first stanza sets the feeling of expectancy as a group approaches a worship center.

Led by the light
Of faith serenely beaming,
With glowing hearts by His cradle we stand;
So led by light
Of a star seeetly gleaming
Here came the Wise Men from the Orient land.
The King of kings lay thus
in lowly manger.
In all our trials
born to be our friend.
He knows our needs
He guardeth us from danger.

In the chorus, "Fall on your knees" choreographs itself. Then while kneeling, the worshippers have an upward and open expression of listening during "O hear the angel voices." During "O night divine...," the group rises; and on the special high emphasis, the group may be circling with right hands touching and reaching upward. The mood is that of mystery.

Behold your King!
Behold Him lowly bend!
Behold your King!
Your King before Him bend.

WHILE BY MY SHEEP

While by my sheep I watched at
night,
Glad tidings brought an angel bright.

Refrain:
How great my joy,
Great my joy.
Joy, joy, joy!
Joy, joy, joy!
Praise we the Lord in heaven on high.
Praise we the Lord in heaven on high.

Children enjoy an echo song or repetition of a design. The early German carol "While By My Sheep" can be interpreted in various ways: in the design of two concentric circles, in two groups, or in two levels or two areas. Since so much of it is antiphonal, one group may echo a second through a movement and the sustaining of some gesture.

There shall be born, so he did say,
In Bethlehem a Child today.

Refrain

There shall He lie, in manger mean,
Who shall redeem the world from sin.

Refrain

With repetition of "joy," the children will do a lot of experimenting in joyful movements. The "joy" in this carol is close in meaning to "surprising joy" or "something wonderful." Let the children feel this through their mind, soul, and body — through the eyes and mouth and the lift of diaphragm and the head — with a quick in-breathing, before singing the words. In this way, hearts are lifted to the Lord.

Lord, evermore to me be nigh,
Then shall my heart be filled with joy!

Refrain

GO TELL IT ON THE MOUNTAIN

While shepherds kept their watching
O'er silent flocks by night,
Behold throughout the heavens
There shone a holy light.

Refrain:
Go, tell it on the mountain,
Over the hills and everywhere,
Go, tell it on the mountain
That Jesus Christ is born.

"Go Tell It On the Mountain" is a jubilant Christmas spiritual with a dynamic start for the group in the opening line of the chorus. After the chorus, during the stanza, one or two dancers may carry the mood while the others remain still, perhaps kneeling. This carol appeals to those who like to run and jump with its energetic emphasis.

The shepherds feared and trembled
When lo! above the earth
Rang out the angel chorus
That hailed our Savior's birth.

Refrain

Down in a lowly manger
The humble Christ was born,
And God sent us salvation
That blessed Christmas morn.

There is a place for a leap and running during "Go tell it on the mountain, over the hills and everywhere! Go tell it on the mountain." Then comes the amazing news "that Jesus Christ is born!" The music seems to stress "Jesus Christ," so the last part of the phrase could express quiet wonder. The general pattern should be worked out according to the space and the decision of the group.

Refrain

Margaret Taylor is the author of numerous books on the history and contemporary practice of dance in worship. She has led dance in worship in over 400 churches in this country and abroad. Having served as International President of the Sacred Dance Guild, she was recently honored by the establishment of the "Margaret Taylor Endowment for Dance in Worship and Education" at Pacific School of Religion, Berkeley. Her books most related to Christmas Carol Dancing include: *A Time to Dance: Symbolic Movement in Worship* and recently *Dramatic Dance With Children In Worship and Education*. She continues to lead workshops across the country as she travels from her home in Oberlin, Ohio.

5 Moving To Carols In Liturgy

Dance and movement as forms and expression of prayer, within the liturgy and without, are still foreign to many people. Christmas time and the singing of Christmas carols afford a good opportunity to introduce movement for those unaccustomed to it, because of the warm, joyous and open feelings elicited by the singing of carols.

Christmas carols are both secular and sacred hymns that appeal to all ages and groups of people. Even people who say they cannot sing enjoy carols and usually wind up joining in. The simplicity and directness of carols gives expression to feelings that can be understood and shared by all. Christmas is a festive season of emotional depth untainted by tragedy or foreboding. The singing of carols during this season gives free expression to our loves, joys, generosity, and hopes. For this reason, Christmas carols have remained spontaneous and fresh, and bring one more in touch with the interdependence among individuals, family, friends, and community.

Traditionally, a carol was a dance and was meant to be danced in a line or circle. In bringing dance back to carols, the whole person will begin to be involved in prayer, individual and communal. The movements added to carols can be simple gestures done by a chorus or by all without detracting from the simplicity of the movements or preventing anyone from participating. Following are a few suggestions for the use of movement in the singing of carols at a Christmas Eve gathering. The singing of carols can sometimes be enhanced by an antiphonal effect created by the alternate singing of a choir and another larger group. So also can choral and congregational dance movements be added.

The choice of the first carol can set the mood for the whole service. "O Come, All Ye Faithful" is well suited as an entrance because it evokes a mood of solemnity and majesty. It is an ideal carol for those unaccustomed to dance. For a church liturgy, a procession could begin, led by the minister outside or in the back of the church.

O COME, ALL YE FAITHFUL
Latin Hymn of the 18th Century

O come, all ye faithful,
Joyful and triumphant
O come ye, O come ye to Bethlehem,
Come and behold Him
Born the King of angels;

The congregation proceeds in a slow even walk up the aisle to their seats, and during the refrain all raise both hands in unison in a gesture of praise.

Refrain:
O come let us adore Him,
O come let us adore Him,
O come let us adore Him,
Christ the Lord.

Sing, choirs of angels,
Sing in exultation,
Sing, all ye citizens of heav'n above:
Glory to God
In the highest;

Refrain

Since "O come, let us adore him" is repeated three times, the arms would be raised a little higher each time. On the words "Christ, the Lord," the hands can be raised again, this time with each person holding the hands of the next person. The effect of this procession could be further enhanced by beginning with the church in darkness, with some in the congregation carrying lighted candles into the church. Gradually as the congregation is seated, the inside lights can be turned on and the candles extinguished.

Yea, Lord, we greet Thee,
Born this happy morning;
Jesus to Thee be glory giv'n,
Word of the Father
Now in flesh appearing;

Refrain

In her book *The Spirit Moves*, Carla DeSola has suggested a movement for the chorus of "O Come All Ye Faithful" which is built on the threefold repetition of the phrase "O come let us adore Him"; the priest leading the procession bows the first time it is sung, the whole procession bows as the phrase is repeated, and the whole congregation bows as it is sung the third time.

For a livelier and gayer, but not necessarily less solemn entrance, "Deck the Halls" might be used. In this case the congregation would already be seated and the dance/movement procession done by the minister and a movement choir.

DECK THE HALLS
Traditional Welsh Melody

Deck the halls with boughs of holly,
Fa, la, la, la, la, la, la, la.
'Tis the season to be jolly,
Fa, la, la, la, la, la, la, la.
Don we now our gay apparel,
Fa, la, la, la, la, la, la, la.
Troll the ancient Yuletide carol,
Fa, la, la, la, la, la, la, la.

See the blazing Yule before us,
Fa, la, la, la, la, la, la, la.
Strike the harp and join the chorus,
Fa, la, la, la, la, la, la, la.
Follow me in merry measure,
Fa, la, la, la, la, la, la, la.
While I tell of Yuletide treasure,
Fa, la, la, la, la, la, la, la.

Fast away the old year passes,
Fa, la, la, la, la, la, la, la.
Hail the new, ye lads and lasses,
Fa, la, la, la, la, la, la, la.
Sing we joyous all together,
Fa, la, la, la, la, la, la, la.
Heedless of the wind and weather,
Fa, la, la, la, la, la, la, la.

While the congregation sings, the minister walks up the aisle to the altar, with the movement choir entering from different directions towards the altar. As the music is lively, the members of the movement choir could skip, leap, or run in, or use some variation which has been choreographed beforehand. Each dancer would enter carrying some flowers, evergreens, or candles with which to decorate the altar. When the minister arrives at the altar, several of the dancers could then enter with vestments and solemnity and ceremoniously dress the minister for the liturgy. Again, this entrance could begin with the church in darkness with the congregation holding lighted candles, and as the carol progresses, gradually the lights of the church would be turned on.

Another choral movement procession could occur at the preparation of gifts to the carol, "We Three Kings."

WE THREE KINGS

We three kings of Orient are;
Bearing gifts we traverse afar,
Field and fountain, moor and
mountain,
Following yonder star.

Refrain:
O star of wonder, star of night,
Star with royal beauty bright,
Westward leading, still proceeding,
Guide us to Thy perfect light.

Born a King on Bethlehem's plain,
Gold I bring, to crown Him again,
King forever, ceasing never,
Over us all to reign.

Refrain

Frankincense to offer have I,
Incense owns a Deity nigh,
Pray'r and praising, all men raising,
Worship Him God most High.

Refrain

Myrrh is mine, its bitter perfume
Breathes a life of gathering gloom;
Sorrowing, sighing, bleeding, dying,
Seal'd in the stonecold tomb.

Refrain

Glorious now behold Him arise,
King and God and sacrifice;
Alleluia, Alleluia,
Earth to the heav'ns replies.

Refrain

The procession would begin simply with one member of the congregation slowly walking up the aisle to the altar with a lighted candle. Behind him would be another person bearing a burning censor. In solemn, gentle movements, this person could swing and twirl the censor in different directions and even overhead, as he proceeds up the aisle. Behind, walking with an even steady pace would be three persons bearing the gifts. As these three persons walk, they could improvise gestures, raising the gifts above their heads. Depending on the comfort with movement of each person, the procession could simply involve walking straight forward with simple arm gestures. Or, more intricately, whole body turns, bows, dipping, gliding, and other movements could be used. This procession is most effective when all five persons walk in tempo, with the candle person just walking and the other four persons improvising their own movements up the aisle.

For a joyous proclamation done with energy and gusto by the whole congregation, try "Angels We Have Heard On High." This may take time explaining and practicing, but will prove to be fun and exciting. Begin by dividing the group into two parts, and these halves into two parts again, so that there are four sections in all. There are only three movements involved: 1) from sitting to standing, 2) a trumpet-like gesture, with one hand to the mouth as if shouting, and the other arm outstretched high on a diagonal, and 3) a raising of both arms high above the head. These movements are all done to the refrain, "Gloria in excelsis Deo."

ANGELS WE HAVE HEARD ON HIGH

Angels we have heard on high,
Sweetly singing o'er the plains,
And the mountains in reply
Echoing their joyous strains:

The carol is begun sitting down.

Refrain:
Gloria in excelsis Deo,
Gloria in excelsis Deo.

On the first musical descant of "Gloria" the first section jumps up to standing with arms in the trumpet gesture facing in another direction; and similarly with the other two groups — all four groups facing different directions.

Shepherds, why this jubilee?
Why these songs of happy cheer?
What great brightness did you see?
What glad tiding did you hear?

On the words "in excelsis Deo," each group faces the others with both arms raised high, and gradually they all lower both arms.

Refrain

The second "Gloria in excelsis Deo" is repeated similarly, only without jumping up this time, and the final lowering of arms is done with everyone facing front. People then sit down to repeat the next stanza.

Another carol for a large group would be at the "Kiss of Peace," perhaps using "God Rest Ye Merry, Gentleman." Again, the movement would be done on the refrain with the people divided into two sections.

GOD REST YE MERRY, GENTLEMEN

God rest ye merry, gentlemen,
Let nothing you dismay,
For Jesus Christ, our Savior,
Was born upon this day,
To save us all from Satan's pow'r
When we were gone astray:

Refrain:
O tidings of comfort and joy,
Comfort and joy,
O tidings of comfort and joy.

On the first "O tidings of comfort and joy, comfort and joy," each half would greet the other group with some gesture of blessing and greeting.

From God, our Heavenly Father,
A blessed angel came,
And unto certain shepherds
Brought tidings of the same,
How that in Bethlehem was born
The son of God by name:

Refrain

The shepherds at these tidings,
Rejoiced much in mind,
And left their flocks a feeding
In tempest, storm and wind,
And went to Bethlehem straightway,
The Blessed Babe to find:

Refrain

On the second "O tidings..." the members would then turn to those around them in their own section and repeat the same gesture. A variation on this would be to sing the first stanza of the carol and refrain four times, each time changing the word "gentlemen" to "gentlefolk," "littlefolk," and "friends." For each repetition, only that group mentioned would do the greeting, until the last time all would join in on the "friends" section. The gesture executed could be planned beforehand or improvised, probably depending on how comfortable everyone is with dance and movement.

Another example is "O Come, O Come, Emmanuel," which could be used as a congregation recesses out of church.

O COME, O COME, EMMANUEL

O come, O come, Emmanuel,
And ransom captive Israel,
That mourns in lonely exile here,
Until the Son of God appear.

Refrain:
Rejoice! Rejoice! Emmanuel,
Shall come to thee,
O Israel!

O come, thou dayspring, come and
cheer,
Our spirits by thine advent here;
Disperse the gloomy clouds of night,
And death's dark shadows put to
fight.

On the refrain, as everyone sings, "Rejoice!" hands are clapped together and the motion is continued by raising the arms in front of the body as high as possible, and then opening them out to the side. This is done to each "Rejoice!" Finally, on "Emmanuel shall come to thee, O Israel," grasp the hands of the next person, so that both arms and voices are raised to the rafters.

Refrain

O come, thou wisdom from on high,
And order all things, far and nigh
To us the path of knowledge show,
And cause us in her ways to go.

Refrain

O come, desire of nations, bind
All peoples in one heart and mind;
Bid envy, strife and quarrels cease;
Fill the whole world with heaven's
peace.

Refrain

These are some examples of what can be done with carols in terms of dance and movement. They are not meant to be followed exactly as outlined here, but as a suggestion of what may be done. Some are choreographed and others are improvised. There are thousands of Christmas carols, some quite beautiful but relatively unknown. Large group movements should be used with the well known carols, while lesser known carols can be used for movement choirs that have the time to rehearse and become familiar with older and lesser known carols. In the season of Christmas as well as throughout the year, the important thing in doing liturgical dance, whether choreographed or improvised, is to allow the spirit to flow through us and become spontaneously creative, joyous and sharing.

Carla DeSola directs the Omega Dance Company in residence at the Cathedral of St. John the Divine in New York City. A graduate of the Julliard School, Carla writes the regular dance column in *Liturgy* Magazine, teaches courses on "worship and dance" at New York Theological Seminary, summer courses at Pacific School of Religion, Berkeley, and is the author of the recent book *The Spirit Moves: A Handbook for Dance In Prayer.*

Peter Madden works with the Omega Dance Company and writes up reports of the Omega Company dances.

6 Updating Christmas Carols To Jazz

The original carols were dances of celebration which were popular during the 12-14th centuries. Accompanied by songs and consisting of simple steps that were contemporary to the day, the carols were simple in form and required no partners. Thus everyone could perform them at church festivals and social affairs.

One version, the *branle*, was done in a ring with steps arranged so that the circle progressed in one direction (left) and stressed teamwork. In contrast, the *farandole* wound through narrow streets using a greater variety of figures and allowed the different age groups to perform steps which appealed to them. Without a doubt, these dances reflected the life and times of the dancers.

Today carol dancing has returned to our homes and our churches, especially at Christmas time. Often the current performances have been re-creations of what might have been done in medieval days. But times have changed — along with dance steps and social customs. It is time to update our carol dances, time to add a touch of today and make them once again contemporary with the times in which they are danced.

Non-partner and line dances have been popular social forms for several decades and these types are very adaptable for use in processional line dances, and up front in the chancel of a church. If more space is available, the same sequences can be performed in a circle. Thus, while contemporary, new carols can maintain a direct link to their medieval ancestors.

What steps can be used to update the carols? Modern jazz sequences derived from ballroom, Latin, rock and show styles can be put to both traditional and modern Christmas songs to give a contemporary flavor which is appealing to dancers and congregations alike. Stressing the rhythmical footwork and distinctive use of the arms and hands while downplaying the hip isolations and pelvic movements will decrease the suggestive connotations of this style to which some individuals might object. However, we no longer wear Victorian clothing. We do not use the horse and buggy or model T for transportation. We're living in the 20th century, so let's allow our church festivals and dancers be contemporary in our lives.

The following sequences have been created as recreational jazz dances; that is, simple combinations derived from jazz styles, ones which can be repeated in the manner of a folk dance. Some reverse sides in their repetition, others do not. Some can be adapted to move down an aisle or path, or to move about in larger hall or church. Emphasis is upon locomotor movements, as in the original carols. While some motions may be symbolic, interpretive choreography has in general been left for the dances presented by more experienced performers.

Choreography for three specific carols concludes the chapter. First are two examples of jazz steps set to well known, traditional Christmas songs. Second, choreography is created for one original, contemporary carol written in the current idiom of "pop" music.

JAZZ STEPS

Two Step or Chasse — Step, together, step. Rhythm — quick, quick, slow or 1 and 2. Can be done in any direction or turning.

Jazz Square — Cross right foot over left, step back left, step to right with right foot, step forward left. Rhythm — even; 1, 2, 3, 4.

Lindy — Two step to right (right, together with left, right), rock weight back onto left foot, shift weight forward to right. Rhythm — 1 and 2, 3, 4. Reverses sides in repetition.

Pas de Bourree — Cross right foot behind left, step to left with left foot, cross right foot over in front of left. Rhythm — 1, 2, 3, (hold 4). Can also be done in a back turn, pivoting the body clockwise on the first step with the right foot.

Ball-Change — With weight on right foot quickly shift weight back onto left foot placed next to right heel, return weight to right foot. Rhythm — quick, slow; and 1.

JAZZ ARM AND HAND POSITIONS

Jazz Hand — Fingers spread wide apart. Usually done with palms facing forward.

High V — Arms raised high over head, elbows straight, palms forward and hands further apart than shoulders.

High Right — Move high V to right but not so far that left arm hides face.

In, Down, Up, Out — Bring both hands to chest, palms in and fingers together, elbows to side at shoulder height; drop elbows down so fingers point up; stretch arms up with palms still toward body; turn palms out and press arms down to second position (arms to side at shoulder). Rhythm — 1, 2, 3, 4.

JAZZ SEQUENCES

1. Step right, touch left foot (no weight), step left, touch right foot. 1, 2, 3, 4.
Step side right, cross left foot behind, step side right, close with left foot, 1, 2, 3, 4.
This step can be done around a circle. It can also be done in a square by turning ¼ to the right on the close step. Four repetitions will return dancer to starting position. It can be done processing down an aisle by facing front on the step touch, turning ¼ left so the first step to the side with the right foot is down the aisle, the left foot crosses behind and down the aisle, and the next step is down the aisle again with right foot, turning ¼ right on the close to again face down the aisle.

2. Lindy to right, 1 and 2, 3, 4.
Step left, kick right, ball-change right, left, kick right 1, 2 and 3, 4.
Step right, circle left toes forward on floor, step left, circle right toes forward, 1, 2, 3, 4.
Jazz square starting right over left, back left, side right, forward left, 1, 2, 3, 4.

3. Pas de bourree starting right behind left, side left, cross right in front, touch left, 1, 2, 3, 4.
Step back left in relevee, close right in relevee, step forward left flat foot, close right flat foot. (Reverses in repeat.) 1, 2, 3, 4.

4. Slow step forward right, slow step forward left, 1 — 2, 3 — 4.
Step back right in relevee, close left in relevee and turning ¼ left, step forward right flat foot in new direction, step forward left flat foot. (Do four times to complete square.) 1, 2, 3, 4.

5. Step side right, close left, side right, close left. 1, 2, 3, 4.
Step side right, cross left over in front, step side right, touch left to side. 1, 2, 3, 4.

6. Step in place right, touch left, two — step left, right, left. 1, 2, 3 and 4.
Pas de bouree turning back clockwise but moving to left (right, left, right), step side left. (Done in a circle, this moves continously counter clockwise.) 1, 2, 3, 4.

7. Step forward right, circle left toes forward, step forward left, close right. 1, 2, 3, 4.
Step side left in relevee, step side right in relevee, step left under body (first position) flat foot, close right flat foot. 1, 2, 3, 4.

8. Step right in place, push left (or dig left heel) into floor, step left, dig right heel. Push the opposite fist down on the heel dig. 1, 2, 3, 4.
Step right (hands to chest, elbows out, palms down), touch left (stretch hands to side), step left (hands in), touch right (hands out). 1, 2, 3, 4.

JOY TO THE WORLD
(Processional Dedicated to the Memory of Dr. James A. Smith)

Joy to the world
The Lord is come.
Let earth receive her king.
Let every heart
Prepare Him room,

Step No. 1 moving down the aisle.

Repeat above 8 counts.
Pony (leap right, rock weight forward left, rock weight back to right) starting right, left, right, left making full turn clockwise.

And heaven and nature sing,

Step side right, close left, step side right, touch left.

And heaven and nature sing,
And heaven and heaven

Repeat starting left.
Leap forward right (jazz hands high, isolate left shoulder forward), close left (isolate right shoulder), repeat.

And nature sing.

Leap forward right (isolate left shoulder), step back left (arms down), step side right (jazz hands to side shoulder height).

58

GOOD CHRISTIAN MEN REJOICE

Good Christian men, rejoice,   Lindy starting right and rocking forward and then back to place.

With heart and mind and voice;   Repeat to the left.

Give ye heed to what we say: Step side right (right jazz hand to side), close left (right hand to shoulder), step side right (right jazz hand forward chest high), close left (right hand to shoulder).

New, news!   Step right to side (right jazz hand high), step left to side (left jazz hand high).

Jesus Christ is born today!   Plie and close right to left (circle hands up, cross over, down and out — palms turning in to body and finishing facing out), straighten knees (hands to shoulders and push up).

Ox and ass before him bow,   Step back left, plie left and touch right heel, step back right, plie right and touch left heel.

And He is in the stable now,   Step side left, close right, step side left, touch right.

Christ is born today!   Step diagonally forward right, clap hands, step diagonally forward left, clap hands.

Christ is born today!   Repeat step claps.

GLORY BE TO GOD IN THE HIGHEST

Gary Illingworth
second verse by Joan Huff

Glo-ri-a _____ to God in _____ the high-est! _____

Glo-ri-a _____ to God in _____ the high-est! _____

Glo-ry be to God and on the earth, peace, good-will!

1. One star-ry night not long a-go in the
2. In fields the shep-herds saw the star call-ing

1. shift-ing sands of time up on the earth the
2. them to Beth-le-hem. So to the man-ger

1. child was born who caus-es bells to chime, His
2. they did come to seek this gift from heav'n. Three

1. name was Je-sus, God's own Son, and
2. wise men journ-eyed far to kneel be-

60

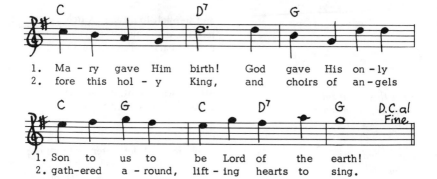

1. Ma - ry gave Him birth! God gave His on - ly
2. fore this hol - y King, and choirs of an - gels

1. Son to us to be Lord of the earth!
2. gath-ered a - round, lift - ing hearts to sing.

GLORY BE TO GOD IN THE HIGHEST

Gloria to   Two-step forward right, left, right, walk back left, right. Swing arms to high right and down.

God in the   Two-step forward left, right, left, walk back right, left. Swing arms to high left and down.

highest.
(Repeat)   Step right to 2nd, left to 2nd, step right 1st, left 1st. Right arm high V, left arm high V, arms down.

Glory be to God
and on the   Two-step right, left, right; left, right, left; right, left, right; left, right, left; turning clockwise. Arms swing to same side as two-step (right, left, right, left).

earth — peace, good will.   Step right to 2nd. Arms to 2nd, isolate right shoulder forward and back, cross both wrists shoulder height in front palms down.

One starry night not
long ago, in the   Step forward right, back left, right, close right (quick), forward right.

shifting sands of time,   Two-step side left, right, left, step forward right, pivot counterclockwise

61

and step left to upstage. Circle palms left, up, over and left, arms high, and over to back wall on pivot step.

upon this earth the child was born, who

Step forward right, two-step side left, right, left, rock back right.

causes bells to chime. His

Rock forward left, step side right, touch left by right heel, step left 2nd. Arms to 2nd (on side step). Hands to chest, palms down, elbows out, arms 2nd.

name was Jesus, God's own son, and Mary gave him birth; God

(Repeat steps from beginning of verse, i.e., step forward, back, back, close forward, two-step, forward and pivot to end facing downstage.)

gave His only Son to us to

Step forward right, two-step side left, right, left step forward right. Circle palms left, up over and left, raise arms forward, elbows bent palms to face.

be Lord of the

Plie right, step back left in relevee. Bow head, raise head and raise arms to high V.

earth

Close right to left in relevee, lower heels. Lower arms through 2nd to sides.

Gloria to God in the highest

Repeat Gloria to God, second verse, and finish with Gloria to God.

Joan Huff is professor of physical education and director of the dance studies at the State University of New York, College at Oswego. She is a member and national director of the Sacred Dance Guild and both choreographs and performs sacred dances. Compositions in this chapter are by Gary Illingworth, a deputy sheriff in Oswego County and student at College at Oswego. He has been accompanist for Aretha Franklin, arranger of music for Tommy James and the Fifth Dimension and composer of several modern religious songs.

7 A Carol Choreography Workbook

Now you try it. Whether you prefer elaborate jazz choreography or simple group dances, the following additional carols are presented for you to "choreograph" yourself. The space on the right is for your notes — when you hit upon a design that you wish to remember.

See the bibliography at the end of this book and the chapter notes throughout for more carols and for more information about liturgical dance.

AWAY IN A MANGER
Text by Martin Luther, melody from a German Folk-Song

Away in a manger,
No crib for a bed,
The little Lord Jesus
Lay down his sweet head;
The stars in the sky
Looked down where He lay,
The little Lord Jesus,
Asleep on the hay.

The cattle are lowing,
The poor Baby wakes,
But little Lord Jesus
No crying He makes,
I love Thee, Lord Jesus!
Look down from the sky,
And stay by my cradle,
Till morning is nigh.

Be near me, Lord Jesus,
I ask Thee to stay,
Close by me forever,
And love me, I pray;
Bless all the dear children
In Thy tender care,
And take us to heaven,
To live with Thee there.

SILENT NIGHT
German words by Joseph Mohr, melody by Franz Gruber

Silent night, Holy night,
All is calm, all is bright,
Round yon Virgin Mother and Child,
Holy Infant so tender and mild,
Sleep in heavenly peace,
Sleep in heavenly peace.

Silent night, Holy night,
Shepherds quake at the sight.
Glories stream from heaven afar,
Heav'nly hosts sing Alleluia;
Christ the Savior is born,
Christ the Savior is born.

Silent night, Holy night,
Son of God, love's pure light
Radiant beams from Thy holy face,
With the dawn of redeeming grace,
Jesus, Lord, at Thy birth,
Jesus, Lord, at Thy birth.

JINGLE BELLS

Folk song, tune by James Pierpont

Dashing through the snow,
In a one horse open sleigh,
O'er the fields we go,
Laughing all the way;
Bells on bobtail ring,
Making spirits bright,
What fun it is to ride
And sing a sleighing song tonight.

Chorus
Jingle bells, Jingle bells,
Jingle all the way!
Oh, what fun it is to ride in
A one horse open sleigh!
Jingle bells, Jingle bells,
Jingle all the way!
Oh, what fun it is to ride in
A one horse open sleigh!

THE FIRST NOWELL
Words traditional, to a traditional English melody

The first nowell the angel did say
Was to certain poor shepherds
In fields as they lay;
In fields where they lay keeping their
sheep,
On a cold winter's night that was so
deep.

Chorus:
Nowell, Nowell, Nowell, Nowell,
Born is the King of Israel.

They looked up and saw a star
Shining in the East,
Beyond them far,
And to the earth it gave great light,
And so it continued both day and
night.

Chorus

This star drew nigh to the northwest,
O'er Bethlehem it took its rest,
And there it did both stop and stay
Right over the place where Jesus lay.

Chorus

Then enter'd in those wisemen three,
Full rev'rently upon their knee,
And offer'd there,
In His presence,
Their gold and myrrh and
frankincense.

Chorus

HARK! THE HERALD ANGELS SING
Words by Charles Wesley, tune by Mendelssohn

Hark! the herald angels sing,
"Glory to the newborn King!
Peace on earth, and mercy mild,
God and sinners reconciled."
Joyful all ye nations, rise,
Join the triumph of the skies;
With th'angelic host proclaim,
Christ is born in Bethlehem!

Hark! the herald angels sing,
"Glory to the newborn King!"

Christ, by highest heav'n adored;
Christ, the everlasting Lord;
Late in time behold Him come,
Offspring of the favored one.
Veiled in flesh the Godhead see;
Hail th'Incarnate Deity,
Pleased as man with men to dwell,
Jesus our Emmanuel!

Hark! the herald angels sing,
"Glory to the newborn King!"

Mild He lays His glory by,
Born that man no more may die,
Born to raise the sons of earth,
Born to give them second birth.
Risen with healing in His wings,
Light and life to all He brings,
Hail, the Sun of Righteousness!
Hail, the heavenborn Prince of Peace!

Hark! the herald angels sing,
"Glory to the newborn King!"

O CHRISTMAS TREE

A traditional German tune

O Christmas Tree, O Christmas Tree,
Your branches green delight us.
O Christmas Tree, O Christmas Tree,
Your branches green delight us.
They're green when summer days are
bright;
They're green when winter snow is
white.
O Christmas Tree, O Christmas Tree,
Your branches green delight us.

O Christmas Tree, O Christmas Tree,
You give us so much pleasure!
O Christmas Tree, O Christmas Tree,
You give us so much pleasure!
How oft at Christmastide the sight,
O green fir tree, gives us delight!
O Christmas Tree, O Christmas Tree,
You give us so much pleasure!

IT CAME UPON A MIDNIGHT CLEAR
Words by Edmund H. Sears, melody by Richard S. Willis

It came upon a midnight clear,
That glorious song of old,
From angels bending near the earth,
To touch their harps of gold:
"Peace on the earth, good will to men,
From heaven's all gracious King;"
The world in solemn stillness lay
To hear the angels sing.

Still through the cloven skies they come,
With peaceful wings unfurled;
And still their heavenly music floats
O'er all the weary world:
Above its sad and lowly plains
They bend on hovering wing;
And ever o'er its Babel sounds
The blessed angels sing.

O ye, beneath life's crushing load,
Whose forms are bending low,
Who toil along the climbing way,
With painful steps and slow.
Look now, for glad and golden hours
Come swiftly on the wing,
O rest beside the weary road,
And hear the angels sing.

For lo! the days are hastening on,
By prophets seen of old,
When with the ever circling years,
Shall come the time foretold,
When the new heaven and earth shall own
The Prince of Peace their King,
And the whole world send back the song
Which now the angels sing.

WHAT CHILD IS THIS?

Traditional words, sung to the traditional English tune "Greensleeves"

What child is this, Who, laid to rest,
On Mary's lap is sleeping?
Whom angels greet with anthems
sweet,
While shepherds watch are keeping?
This, this is Christ the King,
Whom shepherds guard and angels
sing:
Haste, haste to bring Him laud,
The Babe, the Son of Mary!

Why lies He in such mean estate,
Where ox and ass are feeding?
Good Christian, fear: for sinners here
The silent Word is pleading:
Nails, spear, shall pierce Him
through,
The Cross be borne, for me, for you:
Hail, hail the Word made flesh,
The Babe, the Son of Mary!

So bring Him incense, gold and
myrrh,
Come peasant, king, to honor Him,
The King of kings salvation brings,
Let loving hearts enthrone Him.
Raise, raise the song on high,
The Virgin sings her lullaby:
Joy, joy for Christ is born,
The Babe, the Son of Mary!

I SAW THREE SHIPS

Traditional English carol

I saw three ships come sailing in,
On Christmas Day, on Christmas
Day;
I saw three ships come sailing in,
On Christmas Day in the morning.

And what was in those ships all three,
On Christmas Day, on Christmas
Day?
And what was in those ships all three,
On Christmas Day in the morning?

The Virgin Mary and Christ were
there,
On Christmas Day, on Christmas
Day;
The Virgin Mary and Christ were
there,
On Christmas Day in the morning.

Pray, whither sailed those ships all
three,
On Christmas Day, on Christmas
Day;
Pray, whither sailed those ships all
three,
On Christmas Day in the morning?

O they sailed into Bethlehem,
On Christmas Day, on Christmas
Day;
O they sailed into Bethlehem,
On Christmas Day in the morning,

And all the bells on earth shall ring,
On Christmas Day, on Christmas
Day;
And all the bells on earth shall ring,
On Christmas Day in the morning.

Then let us all rejoice amain,
On Christmas Day, on Christmas
Day;
Then let us all rejoice amain,
On Christmas Day in the morning.

WE WISH YOU A MERRY CHRISTMAS

This is a three part round, with melody by Willys Peck Kent, and words by Emma Mueden.

We wish you a merry Christmas and a
happy New Year,
With a pocketful of money and a
cellarful of beer,
And a good fat pig to last you all the
year!

MARY HAD A BABY
Traditional spiritual from the Georgia Sea Islands

Mary had a baby, (Oh, Lord)
Mary had a baby, (Oh, my Lord)
Mary had a baby, (Oh, Lord)
The people keep a-coming and the
train done gone.

Where did she lay him? (Oh, Lord)
Where did she lay him? (Oh, my
Lord)
Where did she lay him? (Oh, Lord)
The people keep a-coming and the
train done gone.

Laid him in a manger (Oh, Lord)
Laid him in a manger (Oh, my Lord)
Laid him in a manger (Oh, Lord)
The people keep a-coming and the
train done gone.

What did she name him? (Oh, Lord)
What did she name him? (Oh, my
Lord)
What did she name him? (Oh, Lord)
The people keep a-coming and the
train done gone.

Named him King Jesus (Oh, Lord)
Named him King Jesus (Oh, my
Lord)
Named him King Jesus (Oh, Lord)
The people keep a-coming and the
train done gone.

Angels sang around him (Oh, Lord)
Angels sang around him (Oh, my
Lord)
Angels sang around him (Oh, Lord)
The people keep a-coming and the
train done gone.

Who heard the singin'? (Oh, my
Lord)
Who heard the singin'? (Oh, Lord)
The people keep a-coming and the
train done gone.

Shepherds heard the singin' (Oh, Lord)
Shepherds heard the singin' (Oh, my Lord)
Shepherds heard the singin' (Oh, Lord)
The people keep a-coming and the train done gone.

Star kept a-shinin' (Oh, Lord)
Star kept a-shinin' (Oh, my Lord)
Star kept a-shinin' (Oh, Lord)
The people keep a-coming and the train done gone.

part two
Designs For Dance Choirs And Companies

8 Dancing "The Ceremony of Carols"

In 1965 Vera Tilson, music director of the Arlington, Virginia Unitarian Church, introduced me to Benjamin Britten's "Ceremony of Carols," a suite of eleven songs with a harp interlude. I fell in love with this music at once and eagerly accepted the commission to choreograph a group dance as part of the Christmas church festival. I appreciated especially Britten's tradition-consciousness, his ability to use ancient and medieval English music styles to create something new. I personally believe very strongly that, particularly during religious celebrations, we should be aware of our cultural heritage as well as our present time.

I had danced in the Arlington Church before; therefore I felt at home with its special peculiarities and took full advantage of them. I used eleven adult dance students and one child for the original presentation. Later, when Bill Akers, music director of St. John's Episcopal Church in Georgetown wanted us to dance it in his church, I gave the choreography to eight members of my professional dance company including a striking male dancer. Since then we have performed it in many places, including churches of all denominations.

My choreography was influenced by the mood of the music and poetry. Yet I never attempted to follow literally the words of the carols. My aim was to express with my choreography the different emotions of Christmas: the anticipation, the joy and jubilation, the inner peace and quiet, the tenderness and loving care, the contrast between an icy, dangerous surrounding world and a sheltered refuge within, and also a prayer, hope, glorification and exultation. I also used symbolism. During a harp interlude, for example, a dancer desperately looks and searches for something all over the church, under pews, up the windows and posts, behind pulpits and doors. Finally she returns to the sanctuary with a burning candle, cradling it and dancing blissfully around it and finally places the found light on the altar like an offering. We dance in our bare feet. Our costumes are long, festive adaptations of medieval gowns correlative to Benjamin Britten's musical style. My own awareness of our cultural heritage, though, is probably most noticeable during the climax of the suite, the Deo Gratias. There the choreography deliberately reflects the gothic style.

Dancing in so many churches is a great artistic challenge. The inside architecture and space of different churches are hardly ever alike.

Therefore one must continue to be creative, changing or adapting the choreography to the uniqueness of each particular place, becoming aware of every opportunity to make the dances more effective and impressive. Every limitation and obstruction should not be ignored but exploited. I am very fortunate that my company is so open and sensitive to these challenges and never objects to near impossible tasks. The utilization of different levels is especially important, I believe, because they become meaningful as well as effective even if difficult to control and to manipulate. In addition, when most of our American churches were designed, the architects never expected that dance and drama would be part of the the service. Unfortunately, therefore, the sight lines in most churches are very poor, and open performing space is in short supply. For all these reasons, steps, choirstalls, balconies, pulpits, balustrades, pews, window sills, etc. should be used to the utmost.

There is quite a difference between congregational dancing and presentations by professional soloists and groups. The one is comparable to congregational singing. It provides personal expression, gratification and exhilaration, reinforced by the awareness of shared emotions and activity, part of a worshipping group. Christian worship is primarily a group experience. The other is more comparable to the functions of a preacher or an art work. The principal purpose is communication, reaching out to involve the congregation. Personal gratification is there but only as a by-product. The dancer is serving with larger than life movements, emotions and thoughts. The choreograhper must have a high artistic standard. Theatricality and technical bravora for their own sake have no place in liturgical dance. The choreographer also must have an understanding of and sensitivity to the needs and aspirations of the community in order to be successful. You cannot lie in dance. Every insecurity, falsehood or superficiality is at once noticeable.

Since dance represents the whole human being: the body, emotions and the spirit, it is natural that primitive humans worshipped by means of dancing. Now we can be encouraged by the fact that sophisticated, contemporary humans have rediscovered the dance and use it once more for spiritual expression in their sanctuaries.

Erika Thimey directs the Washington Dance Theatre. In 1931, she came to the United States from the Mary Wigman School in Germany. She has contributed much to the start of religious dance, especially in Unitarian Churches. Her professional company shares choreographies frequently in church worship and carefully designs each dance to respond to the architecture and liturgy of the particular church. Widely acclaimed here and abroad, her work in 1935 led ecumenical theologian Douglas Horton to assert, "All the arts ought to be brought back into the church, including interpretive dance as instruments... of worship." She has been a member of the Sacred Dance Guild from its inception.

9 Dancing "A Christmas Carol" And "The Cherry Tree Carol"

These two carols are at opposite ends of the spectrum of our repertoire. "A Christmas Carol" has an expandable cast of twenty to forty people, of varying ages, sizes, shapes, and dancing experience. It is forty minutes long, highly dramatic, and uses a supercharged orchestral score. "Cherry Tree Carol" is diminutive, six minutes long, with a cast of three skilled dancers. The drama is muted, evoked rather than exhibited, and the accompaniment is a solo singer.

SCENES FROM "A CHRISTMAS CAROL"

In spite of the dour attitude of some sophisticates, having an annual Christmas production can be a very rewarding enterprise. Everyone likes to be in on the inside of one of the year's great occasions; and little ones look forward to stepping into roles vacated by cast members who have graduated or in other ways moved on.

Each year at St. Mark's Episcopal Church on Capitol Hill in Washington DC, we do "Scenes from A Christmas Carol,'" described in the program as "A Christmas pantomine, with dancing, adapted from Dickens' famous story, in which some of the performers play several different roles." In such a heartwarming story, different scenes can be played and different roles can be given more or less emphasis, depending on the dancing experience and maturity of the current cast. This year we have a strong dancer as the nephew and so have given him rendelades, brise voles, grand fouettes battus and other spectacular steps to do. Scrooge is always played by the oldest and meanest member of the company (M. Craighill), the Ghost by the tallest and most awesome male, and Mr. and Mrs. Fezziwig by the most amiable and ingratiating couple. Bob Cratchit is sometimes portrayed by a dancer, sometimes by an actor; but he is always a cheerful and eager appearing soul. Tiny Tim is usually the younger brother of one of the students of our school and thoroughly enjoys being helped and carried about and finally blessing the whole cast.

The music we use is Bartok's Concerto for Orchestra; at first glance seemingly a difficult support but in actuality, for our version, an accompaniment so graphic that it is handled easily by even the youngest dancers. The landmarks for the different scenes are very strong and clear. I adapt each year's version to the cast, since there is more dancing

and more difficult dancing for the advanced dancers and more pantomime and general business and crowd activity for the less experienced. The scenes run as follows:
(all of them are short and tumble one upon the other).

Act I — Prologue

Scene I — Players: Bob Cratchit, clerk, and Ebeneezer Scrooge, his employer, in the office, the night before Christmas.

Both Scrooge and Bob Cratchit are hunched over their desks in a suspended tableau of their separate preoccupations. Scrooge starts counting his money, dropping it, scrambling for it, slapping it back on the desk, becoming more and more agitated, finally pacing the floor in anger, pantomiming the star, the Christmas tree, followed by strong "Bah" gestures. Cratchit shivers and shakes, goes to the window and back, pulls his scarf around him, tries to write; but his hands are too cold. As Scrooge senses the approach of his nephew, he hides his money.

Scene II — Players: Add nephew.

Scrooge's nephew visits and invites Scrooge to the Christmas Feast. The nephew bounds in, trying to be jovial. Scrooge rejects him, but the nephew refuses to be cowed. Nephew entreats him in dance sequences of large movements but is roundly refused by Scrooge. As Cratchit joins the scene, the nephew goes to his knees imploring Scrooge's better nature. Scrooge tumbles over his nephew's knee, chases Cratchit back to his desk, grabs a fireplace broom and sweeps the nephew offstage. Nephew retreats, saluting Scrooge and wishing him well.

Scene III — Players: Add two businessmen.

Two businessmen plead for money to help the poor and needy. The two portly gentlemen appear — proud and solid representatives of the community. They are imploring but also dancing. Scrooge mimics them, refuses them, and finally sweeps them offstage in a rage telling them in bold gestures that the poor can always earn their own keep in the workhouse.

Scene IV — Players: Cratchit, Scrooge, and Ghost.

Scrooge, confronted by the ghost of his former partner, Marley, is made aware of the eternal torment awaiting such mean and miserly creatures as Scrooge. Scrooge, beside himself in his fury, turns on Cratchit, grabs him, shakes him up, shoves him offstage with a resounding clatter, turns and abruptly confronts the Ghost. Scrooge is startled but soon regains his composure and follows the Ghost, who is wafting around the stage, with mimicking and rejecting gestures. When the Ghost rattles his chains

82

Scrooge is taken aback but returns to challenge the Ghost. The Ghost returns the compliment by subtly threatening Scrooge, lifting and throwing him with thinly concealed violence. When the Ghost removes the bandage from his chin, Scrooge is overcome, and goes to the floor, abject and terrified. The Ghost recounts Scrooge's sins to him, points to his future torture, and warns him of the ghostly encounters awaiting him. The Ghost gives him the sign of benediction, picks up his chains, and silently exits. Scrooge rises, runs wildly to the spots of the different scenes enacted by the Ghost, becomes hysterical and falls senseless to the floor.

Act II — The Ghost of Christmas Past

The Ghost conducts a tour, conjuring up scenes of Scrooge's younger days. Scrooge is sleeping restlessly as the Ghost appears. Again he tries to make the vision disappear; but the Ghost jerks him to his feet and imperiously starts him on a tour of his past.

Scene I — Players: Two or three or four children as Scrooge remembers them.

Scrooge is happy and excited recalling the scene of the children throwing snowballs and gamboling freely in their merriment.

Scene II — Players: the boy, Scrooge, and two, three or four clowns.

The clowns are a vision of Scrooge's lonely childhood. The strange memory of the antics of the exotic and flamboyant clowns causes the real Scrooge to recognize himself in the scene, and he sobs on the Ghost's breast.

Scene III — Players: the boy Scrooge and his little sister.

Scrooge, deserted, at boarding school, on Christmas Eve. The very touching scene of Scrooge's little sister (now dead) coming to ease his pain and loneliness by fetching him home for Christmas. The real Scrooge is confused and dumbfounded by these memories.

Scene IV — Players: Mr. Fezziwig, his two apprentices, Mrs. Fezziwig, and guests.

Christmas party at the Fezziwig's, Scrooge's former employer. Mr. Fezziwig interrupts his very important business to summon his two apprentices and command them to make ready for the Christmas festivities. Mrs. Fezziwig arrives with all the employees. A scene of gaiety and good spirits ensues with all dancing a quadrille; and Mr. and Mrs. Fezziwig providing a fancy duet as a special treat. The real Scrooge remembers all this and becomes happy and excited; but the Ghost remains unmoved, imperious and accusing.

Scene IV — Players: Scrooge as a young adult, his fiancee, her husband and daughter.

Scrooge, the suitor, is rejected for his avarice. Scrooge, now a young man and clearly manifesting the greedy and meanspirited side of his nature, is refused by his beloved who tells him he is treading a path she can not follow. The scene ends with a tableau of the girl with the man she does accept, and their child. This happening angers the real Scrooge; and he turns on the Ghost, beats on his chest, and, reaching to the top of his head, squashes him to the floor. He then staggers and falls as he realizes what he has done.

Act III — The Ghost of Christmas Present

The Jolly Ghost of Christmas Present projects possible scenes of Christmas now. Scrooge awakens with a start and is surprised to find the Ghost not there. The Ghost soon appears, in brilliant light, as the Jolly Ghost of Christmas Present. He extends an elaborate welcome to Scrooge and commands him to take his robe and accompany him on another tour.

Scene I — Players: Mrs. Cratchit and children, Martha, Bob Cratchit, Tiny Tim.

The Cratchit family's Christmas dinner. Scrooge and the Ghost arrive at Bob Cratchit's home which the Spirit blesses as they enter. Mrs. Cratchit and the children are busy arranging the house for the Christmas feast. They lace their busywork with dancing and in comes Martha. After warm greetings Martha is hidden away and Bob comes in with Tiny Tim on his shoulder. Much commotion, greetings and dancing. Tiny Tim is carried out, followed in procession by the family. Scrooge protests to the Ghost but the Ghost is more accusatory than before and roughly conducts him to the Christmas party at the nephew's house, again blessing the house before entering.

Scene II — Players: nephew, niece, Topper, niece's sister, and guests.

Christmas party at the nephew's home — making light of Scrooge's refusal to attend. Here the dancing is more formal and is punctuated by pantomime mimicking Scrooge's manners and miserliness. All enjoy the game of Blindman's Bluff with Topper. At the end when all raise a toast, Scrooge attempts to join the party but is abruptly pulled away by the Ghost.

(A short blackout here allows the abject children to place themselves under the Ghost's cloak and the characters for Act IV to take their places.)

Act IV — The Ghost of Christmas Future

The Ghost points to what lies ahead if Scrooge persists in his evil ways.

Scene I — Players: Ghost, Scrooge and children.

The Ghost has shoved Scrooge to center stage where he beholds the abject children crawl and fall from under the Ghost's cloak and beg for his mercy. He at last becomes aware of his baseness, and expresses his torment to the Ghost, pleading to be led on and to be confronted with the full denouement of his life story and deeds.

Scene II — Players: Scrooge as an old man, passersby.

Scrooge, dead and abandoned in the street. Old Scrooge lies dead in the street. Various passersby stumble over him, turn and recognize him, scoff at his fate, yawn, laugh, etc., and kick him and move on. The real Scrooge is perplexed at this scene and asks the Ghost for its meaning. The Ghost, unresponsive, leads him on.

Scene III — Players: Pawnbroker and thieves.

At the pawnshop, his worldly goods, stolen and traded in. The looters arrive with Scrooge's paltry worldly goods and enact an ugly scene. They scramble and argue among themselves and try to force some remuneration from a disgusted and begrudging pawnbroker. The real Scrooge is horrified and revulsed by this scene.

Scene IV — Players: The family as before, and two pallbearers.

Lighting reveals the second scene at Bob Cratchit's home. Mrs. Cratchit and the children sit in a half circle swaying in lament. Tiny Tim is carried in motionless and laid before them. Bob enters, sees his dead son, and breaks down in grief. The pallbearers again appear and carry Tiny Tim off in funeral procession. The real Scrooge is overcome with remorse as the full consciousness of his evil deeds and wicked attitudes dawns upon him. He repents, begs the Ghost's forgiveness and promises to become a new man. The Ghost finally responds with emotion and shakingly gives him the sign of benediction as he retreats offstage.

Act V — Finale

Scrooge does repent and change. He is blessed with a real Christmas amid the scenes and companions of his memories. And Tiny Tim lives to become his good friend and to say, "God Bless Us All."

Players: The Company.

Scrooge awakens with a start to find that all is real, that he has not missed Christmas Day and that he has been awarded the chance to undo the evil results of his malice. He is in such a frantic rush to accomplish all this that he has a terrible and very funny time getting dressed — putting clothes on backwards and upside down and getting all tangled up in them. At last, somewhat straightened out he orders a huge turkey from the apprentices and displays it proudly to all. When the two businessmen appear to beg again he astonishes them by showering them with money, adding the turkey as a bonus donation. Cratchit arrives at the office, terrified and trembling. Scrooge berates him in mock anger. All turns to rejoicing, however, when Scrooge gives him a generous advance on a generous raise in pay.

The whole cast now appears on stage in a highly energetic dance sequence with intricate steps, big jumps and big lifts. This dissolves into a series of flashbacks which Scrooge reacts to with intense interest — the snowball scene with little children, the school scene with the young Scrooge fetched home by his sister, the clown scene, the party at the nephew's home — but this time Scrooge joins in and the guests raise their glasses to him. Then comes the reenactment of the party and dance at the Fezziwig's. Scrooge is invited to join and does so with alacrity. Tiny Tim is placed on Scrooge's shoulders and they do a dance in this fashion. General exuberant dancing follows, ending with a grand company bow. Scrooge and the Ghost appear in back with Tiny Tim on their shoulders. Tiny Tim gives his blessing to cast and audience.

As can be seen, liberties have been taken with the book. The scenes selected to tell the story are the most easily adapted to a nonverbal, visual medium and those requiring a minimum of props and scenery. Another choreographer might handle the story quite differently. In our version the real Scrooge and the Ghost are onstage the whole time after their first entrance and the various incarnations of Scrooge are enacted by different members of the cast. We have a most imaginative lighting technician who, with very meager equipment, manages, through lights, to shift the scenes back and forth between the players and Scrooge and the Ghost, highlighting the most dramatic moments with overhead spots on a darkened stage. "The stage" is the chancel of St. Mark's which is a sizeable open area.

The recording of Bartok's Concerto for Orchestra that we use is George Szell with the Cleveland Orchestra, Columbia recording ML 6215, Stereo MS 6815. We take liberties with the music also, rearranging it somewhat to achieve the desired dramatic effects. Act I uses the first movement in its entirety. Act II uses the second movement in its entirety. Act II uses the fourth movement in its entirety. The transition between Act II and Act IV (the scene of the abject children) starts with the big crash in the middle of the third movement and continues to the end of that movement. Act V uses the fifth movement in its entirety. Some of the dramatic confrontations between the Ghost and Scrooge are played in silence between the acts. The whole production runs about forty minutes.

Costuming is simple. Mainly we use blouses and turtlenecks, long skirts, scarfs and shawls for the women, tights or tight trousers, tuxedo shirts with added puff sleeves and vests for the men. Mob caps and ear muffs complete the attire.

I hope I have provided enough information, dear reader, to get you interested in this project. I think you will find your cast, young and old, genuinely caught up in the story and giving their full cooperation, because it is a tale to soften the hardest of hearts. God bless you all!

CHERRY TREE CAROL

On a much smaller scale, and for inclusion in a Christmas or Epiphany celebration is the Cherry Tree Carol. Lasting six minutes, it is performed by three dancers — the Tree, Mary and Joseph. This dance requires subtlety, sensitivity and delicacy of interpretation on the part of the performers. It does not require sophisticated technique, but only dancers with full control over the nuances of movement can reveal its beauty to the audience.

The dancing very simply follows the story line of the carol, but the quality of movement evokes a feeling of quiet wonder and other worldliness. It is a miniature, pictorially suggesting early medieval paintings of the Nativity. Joseph is a simple man, right-hearted but wrongheaded. Mary is trusting and guileless, forgiving his anger and accusation without acrimony. The whole action revolves around the Tree, which participates vicariously and actually in the drama.

The action is as follows: The Cherry Tree is positioned center stage. Its posture is gnarled and twisted.

I — Joseph walks slowly and stiffly from upstage left to center stage, in front of the Tree. Mary enters with soft triplets from upstage right, circling the Tree. They enact betrothal, she placing her hands on his.

II — They walk in the garden with gliding steps. The discovery of the Tree is communicated by large, slow arm movements and soft clapping of the hands.

III — Mary whispers in Joseph's ear to reach for the cherries because she is with child. This movement is repeated as they walk around the Tree.

IV — Joseph flies in anger, in large, stylized movements, demanding to know the father of the child. Mary moves to the Tree and the Tree gently cradles her.

V — The Cherry Tree quivers and bows down. Mary is filled with awe and joy. Joseph is stupefied and immobilized.

VI — Mary moves around the Tree, gathering cherries, then goes to Joseph and offers her hands to him.

VII — Joseph repents and asks forgiveness. Mary blesses him and they listen as Jesus' birthday is announced in the song.

VIII — The last scene is a series of continuous turns by all three as they spin in wonderment and adoration, made whole again through the miracle of the Cherry Tree.

The dance has an interesting history. It was commissioned by the singer, John Langstaff, and was accompanied live by him as part of his production "Christmas Masques and Revels" which was given at Lisner Auditorium, Washington, DC and at Town Hall, New York City, during the Christmas season of 1957. Ten years later, Christmas 1967, the whole production was remounted for NBC network television and aired on Christmas morning. Last year I went to Boston and set the dance for the Boston company, City Dance Theatre, that John was using for his 1976 revival of the production. Meanwhile we have done many, many performances of the Cherry Tree Carol, to a tape made for us by John Lanstaff. It has become one of the signatures of the St. Mark's Dance Company.

Mary Craighill directs the St. Mark's Dance Company, housed since 1962 in St. Mark's Episcopal Church on Capitol Hill, Washington, DC. Based on some 200 students who study a full range of dance courses in her St. Mark's Dance Studio, she has developed choreographies that have been featured on NBC television as well as programs that have toured east coast churches. She has directed dances for Washington Cathedral, the Folger Shakespeare Library, public service programs in schools, and recently in the Capitol Hill Lunch Theatre series supported by the National Endowment for the Arts Expansion Program. In 1975, she was co-leader with Doug Adams of the National Institute of the Sacred Dance Guild. She took her early dance training with Jose Limon, Valerie Bettis, Kathryn Mulowny and Leon Fokine.

10 A Pageant Of Christmas Carols

By sharing this detailed account of our "Christmas Pageant — Light" (Christ as the light of the world) and through our attempts to link the symbolic with the actual, we hope that people celebrating in churches, schools, auditoriums, even outdoors, can utilize fully or in part our community's ideas and adapt them to each particular space. For further convenience I have divided this chapter into seven segments: physical set-up, publicity, performance groups, props, music, script, and choreography.

Physical set-up (see also drawing on page 93). Our church altar platform (6' by 12') was enlarged by a portable extension of the same dimensions. With the sanctuary doors closed and the portable steps moved forward, we had a suitable stage with three routes of approach: right and left sides and center, each with three steps up to the two foot elevation. With doors behind and on either side of the back of the altar/stage and with the east, west, and north doors, we had five means of actually entering the stable. Our movable individual wooden stacking chairs (sides interlocked when necessary) allow for regulation of aisle space and space in front of the altar/stage. This space then can be used both for worship and for purely social events such as meetings, dances, and dinners, as well as for separate classrooms when the dividing walls are used.

The east loft houses our choir, organ, piano, and a trumpet player for ordinary liturgies. For the pageant we had two more trumpets, trombone, tympani, harpsichord, flute, and guitar as well as the narrator and portable spotlight in this space. Here, too, is where sound and light systems are controlled.

The west loft allows for seating of parishoners, and its elevated rows of seats are especially good viewing places for children, since the ground floor seats are on a flat rather than inclined floor. There is another portable spotlight here.

Over the center of the ground floor are five adjustable permanently mounted white spotlights which focus attention on the altar/stage.

Chairs are placed so that people sit around and in front of the altar/stage to allow for maximum viewing ability.

Publicity (see also reproduction below). We distributed parchment-like scrolls of invitation to family members and also mailed them to the surrounding community by a private postal service (this cost less than mailing through US Post Office) a week before the pageant. As you can see, no one was singled out for credit. Many participants had been members of the Stable Family before I joined, and all felt that the gift was much more important than the identity of the giver.

THE CHURCH OF ST. MAURICE
2851 Stirling Road
Father John C. Mulcahy, Pastor

The family of St. Maurice invites
You and your family to
Christmas at The Stable

LIVING PAGEANT IN SONG,
SACRED DANCE AND DRAMA
DECEMBER 16th, 17th, 18th at 8:00 P.M.

Christmas is a privileged moment in time. It is the point of reference for all that a Christian hopes to become: the starting place for a life of giving... the joy-filled way into the gift of living. Christmas is the glory of God, illuminating the universe. Christmas is an event... a happening... a celebration of love!

Come to the Stable! Return with us to Bethlehem! Hear the pleas and prophecies of God's people! Rejoice as we herald the Good News through glorious pageantry! Dance into the mystery and majesty of the realized Kingdom with the resurrected Christ! Share our joy as we present our annual 'Thank you' gift to the community... Christmas at the Stable!

An Invitation
Come to the Stable

Part I — Prophecy and Promise... All praise this night for the blessings of light... even the heavens are telling the glory of God... the

90

God of the heights!
God of the depths!
Maker of heaven and maker of earth.
Lord, what is man that you should care for him?
Jesus is coming!
Jesus is coming!
Lord Jesus Come!
Come... arise, the glory of God shall live among you... the Babe of Bethlehem!

Part II — Proclamation/Promise Fulfilled... He who is mighty has done great things... we shall dance, dance, wherever we may be... the Lord of the dance leads us... to be counted... to moments of expectation... through disappointment and rejection... to Bethlehem... See his star!
Shining bright!
In the sky this Christmas Night!
Follow me joyfully!
Hurry to Bethlehem
And see the son of Mary!
Gloria! In excelsis Deo... Alleluia, Christ is Born!

Part III — Parousia/The Promise... I am... and will always be... with you... Wander and wonder... search, ask, find... Because God loves you... come join the Lord of the Dance... and
Dance, then
Wherever you may be,
"I am the Lord of the Dance" said he.
"And I'll lead you all
Wherever you may be,
And I'll lead you all in the Dance."
Said he.
Hallelujah! King of Kings and Lord of Lords... this silent night has become a holy night... filling our hearts with joy as we shout that age old greeting... Merry Christmas! Merry Christmas!

As numerous as the stars in the sky are the 'stars' of the Stable! Great thanks and accolades of praise for the children, youth, and adult voices that have made this 'joyful noise unto God'... for script, music, choreography, staging and direction... for love spoken in countless hours of practice... precious time 'borrowed' from this moment of life to enrich the community and breathe the promise of peace... joy... love... to all!

To the nameless multitude...
Thanks and God bless!

Performance groups. Because of our size and diversity and because our pageant was a total family effort, we attempted to employ people from all parish organizations.

Our main characters were Prophets I and II, Caesar Augustus, Mary, Joseph, and the adult Jesus. Prophet I wore an animal skin and carried a gnarled branch for a staff; Prophet II wore a brocade robe. Mary's long white dress was covered with a blue hooded robe, and Joseph wore a plain brown robe. Caesar wore a toga and matching headband. Jesus wore a white robe with a white stole accented with gold. There were three short speaking parts for members of each of the three choirs. The narrator was heard from the choir loft but was not seen; he unified the movement from one section of the action to another.

Children's choir, girls wore dresses and boys wore slacks and shirts, but all wore popover tops of off-white linen-like fabric over their clothing.

Youth choir, grades seven through ten, dressed in jeans and shirts to give a contemporary look to their part.

Adult choir's avocado green robes were accented with off-white stoles with red crosses for Advent (crosses are detachable and changed according to season — white for Easter, purple for Lent, red for Pentecost, green for all other times).

Sacred dancers wore white long sleeved scoop neck leotards, flesh colored footless tights, and ankle length white wrap-around skirts. A forty inch square of opaque fabric in white, yellow, blue, green, pink, or lavender pastel was made into a popover top by cutting a hole in the center to allow for the head; small pieces of elastic at the points which fell over the middle finger on each hand held the top in place, and the points falling just below the waist in front and back gave a covered-up look without restricting movement. The angel wore white for her solo; Mary, the dancer (who was a separate person from Mary in the tableau), added a rectangular piece of cloth for a headwrap to her costume; when all five dancers danced together in interpretation of other music, the angel changed her white top for a yellow one and Mary removed her headpiece.

Props consisted of printed census forms, pencils, small individual candles for all in attendance, one large candle in elaborate holder to symbolize "the light," small wooden manger, wood pillars to simulate pillars (four) of the stable, one bale of hay strewn in manger and around stage to represent further the stable within our stable, and an 18 inch diameter mirrored ball to create sparks of reflected light over cast members and audience at time of the birth.

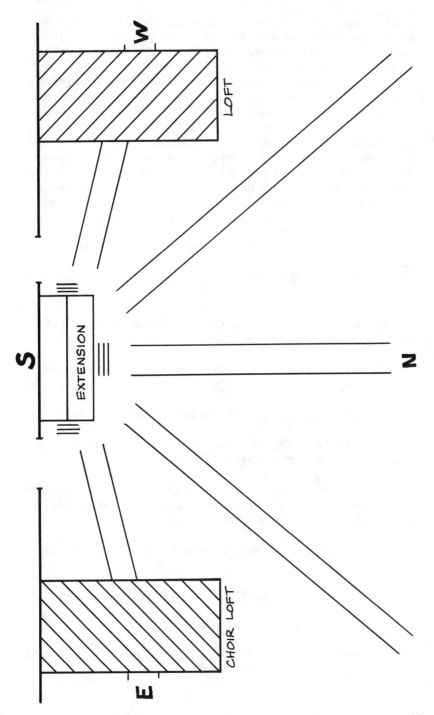

LOFT

EXTENSION

CHOIR LOFT

W

S

N

E

As the audience entered the stable, ushers distributed Caesar Augustus' census forms which requested name, address, and lineage of each family along with pencils to complete them. Many people were confused and put them in pockets and purses, but none hesitated when the blustery Caesar appeared on the west balcony and demanded their return during the pageant. In this manner the audience was drawn into the pageant as participant rather than as mere observer.

Music has always been a large part of all celebrations at St. Maurice, and so there was no problem with audience participation in singing choruses of familiar songs. When Fr. Mulcahy welcomed the audience, he also introduced several Adult Choir members who led the people in rehearsal before the pageant actually began. Music and its sources, when available, are listed next in the order in which they occurred.

"Tallis Canon" (All Praise to Thee, My God, This Night), Thomas Kane.

"The Heavens Are Telling" (Chorus from "The Creation"), Franz Josef Haydn.

"Lord Jesus Come" (from "Lyric Liturgy"), Alexander Peloguin, GIA Publications, Inc., 7404 Mason, Chicago, IL, 60638.

"The Babe of Bethlehem," Folk hymn from *Southern Harmony Shape-Note Hymnal.*

"Do You Hear What I Hear?", Words adapted by Fran Leto.

"Christmas Concerto (Opus 8)," Guiseppe Torelli, Carl Fischer, Inc., 5662 Cooper Square, New York, NY, 10003.

"Lord of the Dance" (from Shaker tune "Simple Gifts"), New words by Sydney Carter, *Sydney Carter: In the Present Tense*, 1963 by Galliard Ltd., Galaxy Music Corp., NY, sole US agent.

"Star Carol," Cat. No. 84.233, Oxford Carols, Oxford University Press, NY.

"Jazz Gloria," Natalie Sleeth, CM 7752, 1970 by Carol Fischer, Inc.

"I Wonder As I Wander," John Jacob Niles.

"Because Your God Loves You," 1977 by C. and R. Avello, 4852 Sheridan Street, Hollywood, FL, 33022.

DO YOU HEAR WHAT I HEAR?
New words by Fran Leto

When the world became lonely and sad
And peoples' lives were empty
Peoples' lives were empty
God the father felt so very bad
And wanted to help us
And wanted so to help us
Wanted so to help us
Wanted to help us
He said he had a plan to make us glad
He would give all the love that he had
He would give all the love that he had.

He sent an angel to a simple maid
And asked if she would trust him
Asked if she would trust him
Could you be God's mother, would you dare?
Would her faith allow her?
Would her faith allow her?
He needs a place to call his very own
And someone to give him a home
And someone to give him a home.

Filled with awe the maiden then replied:
Does he really want me?
Does he really want me?
Maybe I could do it if I tried
And God would surely guide me
God would surely guide me
So the angel sent the spirit from above
Who would help her always to love
And to give life to God's only son.

BECAUSE YOUR GOD LOVES YOU

R. Avello
C. Avello

1. Be-cause your God loves you,_____
2. Just think now you are free_____

1. 𝄍 Be-cause He tru - ly cares,_____
2. for be-liev-ing and fol - l'wing me,_____

1. This then is the reas - on why He
2. As you see be - fore you still, I

1. sent His Son to live and die_____
2. live a - gain and al - ways will._____

1. So that you may one day_____
2. So re - joice my friends,_____to the

1. live with Him in peace._____
2. Fath - er sing your praise._____

1. My walk up - on this earth _____ was a
2. I am with you for - ev - er

nec - es - sar - y grief. _____

till the end _____ of all days. _____

97

Part I

All lights out.

Narrator: In the beginning there was darkness. And God said, "Let there be light!" And the light of God penetrated the darkness.

(Lights on dim.)

Narrator: Then God said, "Let us make man with the light of our own image." And man came forth into the light. And God said, "He is very good and my special light and love shall always be with him. I shall be his father. He shall be my son."

But man began to dim the light by placing God in the sky above, man made God a distant light. A God of Power. A God of Law. The light of God could no longer penetrate the darkness of man. So God planned a re-creation to let himself become the light and be born as man.

(Lights out.)

Meditation.

Narrator: In the silent darkness let us meditate upon our need of light and the joy of receiving the light of God tonight as we say, "Father, send the light of your son into my life." *(Audience repeats this line with narrator.)*

Silence one minute.

(Adult choir silently enters east, west, and north doors with the first person at each entrance lighting the next person's candle, then each choir member lights the candle of an audience member on either side of the aisle; the light is passed on until the entire church is candle lit. The choir then processes in singing a capella "Tallis Canon" until they have formed a background on stage facing audience. Choir blows out candles; audience does same.)

Darkness.

Narrator: Unto this earth, covered with darkness and distress, into the blackness of anguish which led men only deeper into the night; amidst the cold sands of Judah, in a land of deep shadows, the spirit of the Lord came upon Isaiah, proclaiming a time of favor from Yahweh, the Lord of Heaven and Earth.

(Glimmer of light spotted on stage, with dimmer switch up a little for choir to be able to read music. Adult choir sings, "The Heavens Are Telling." At completion of song, lights are dimmed to glow as choir silently exits east and west doors.)

Prophet I: *(entering from east doors)* Let me sing the praises of the goodness of the Lord, and of his marvelous deeds. He has shown us great kindness in his mercy and in his boundless goodness. In his love and pity he redeemed us for himself, he lifted us up an carried us throughout the days of old. But our people rebelled; they turned away from God's presence. Then God turned from his people. *(Moves up onto stage.)* Where is he who endowed Moses with the Holy Spirit, who divided the waters and let us walk through the ocean? Look down from Heaven, look down from your holy dwelling place!

Choir Person *(yells):* How can he see you? Does God have eyes?

Prophet: Where is your might?

Choir Person II: He has no might. What has he done for you?

Prophet: Do not let your compassion go unmoved, for you are our Father.

Choir Person III: What kind of father is he that he leaves his children?

Prophet: Why, Lord, do you leave us to stray from your ways?

Choir Person III: So you agree with me that he has left you?

Prophet: Return for the sake of your servants, Lord! Oh, that you would tear the heavens open and come down!

(Prophet exits quickly out west door.)

(Lights dim as Adult Choir sings "Lord Jesus, Come." Audience joins in on chorus. At completion of song movable spot at west loft shines on north entrance as houselights gradually dim to off. Prophet II enters carrying large candle in elaborate holder. Single drumbeat accents Prophet's procession down center aisle. Three dancers follow him then kneel in aisle as Prophet ascends center steps.)

Prophet II: See, the days are coming when the Lord will make a new covenant with his people. But not a covenant like the one he made with our ancestors; they broke that covenant. This covenant I will make in the days that are coming. Deep within them I will plant my law, writing it in their hearts. Then the Lord will be our God, and we will be his people. "All people will know me says the Lord, the least no less than the greatest, since I will forgive their iniquity and never call their sin to mind."

(Prophet II places candle on floor at front of stage left as dancers walk up center steps to kneel at an oblique angle to right of center stage. Entire stage in bright light.)

Narrator: Arise, shine out, for your light has come, and the glory of the Lord is rising upon you. The darkness that covered the earth so long now is gone, and the glory of the Lord shall live among you. You shall call your walls salvation, and the name of your gates shall be praise. Violence and plunder shall not be heard in your land. The Lord will be your light forever... God will be your glory. Never more will the sun give you daylight, nor the moon shine on you. The Lord will be your everlasting light. Lift your eyes and look around. At this sight you will grow radiant, your hearts throbbing and full. I will make you an eternal pride, and a joy to last forever and ever.

(Adult choir sings "Babe of Bethlehem" verses 1, 4, 5, 6, 7, 8 while dancers interpret lyrics. When song and dance are completed dancers exit west door behind prophet who takes candle with him while last two lines of song are softly played on piano as exit accompaniment.)

Part II

(Stage lights on.)

Narrator: Men are always missing God, for they search for him in the wrong places. They listened for the roar of thunder but could not hear a baby cry. They searched inside the marble halls of kings, but could not stoop to enter a cave. They studied ancient scripture for a clue, but failed to understand the language of their own heart. They talked for hours in heated debate, but could not sit still to listen for a moment in silence. They wanted to love others but forgot to love their own. So God surprised man by coming again in a way not known to us, but we will find him somewhere within ourselves and others if we can still be surprised by faith in a new life.

(Lights out.)

Meditation.

Narrator: Do we try to tell God what he should be, or are we listening for a new voice? Are we willing to find God in our everywhere life? Can we accept ourselves as the sacred place of his birth tonight?

(Children's choir enters singing "Do You Hear What I Hear?" and sits in clusters of three to five to become foreground setting for Angel and Mary scene.)

Narrator: In the sixth month, the angel Gabriel *(Angel enters south door at stage right, white spotlight on her)* was sent from God to a town of Galilee named Nazareth, to a virgin betrothed to a man named Joseph, of the House of David. The virgin's name was Mary *(Mary enters south door at stage left, white spotlight on her)*. Upon arriving, the angel said to her, "Rejoice, O highly favored daughter! The Lord is with you. Blessed are you among women. Do not fear, Mary. You have found favor with God. You shall conceive and bear a son and give him the name Jesus. Great will be his dignity and he will be called Son of the Most High. The Lord God will give him the throne of David his father. He will rule over the House of Jacob forever; and his reign will be without end."

("Christmas Concerto," cut to one minute in length, is played on harpsichord for angel's dance. At completion of dance, angel kneels back stage right as Mary dances to two choruses of "Lord of the Dance" played on piano. At end of Mary's dance both she and angel freeze in tableau while narrator continues.)

Narrator: At Mary's "Yes," salvation began to unfold and envelop mankind. The power of the Most High overshadowed her and she became a Temple, a living Tabernacle encasing the Son of God. *(Chorus of "Lord of the Dance" is played softly on piano as Mary exits west door followed by angel.)* And Mary danced into history, with prophecy beneath her feet and the Promise quickening within her womb. She danced into Elizabeth's arms singing, "My being proclaims the greatness of the Lord, my spirit finds joy in God my savior, for he has looked upon his servant in her lowliness; all ages to come shall call me blessed. God who is mighty has done great things for me... holy is his name!"

(Stage lights dim.)

Narrator: It was during this time that Caesar Augustus published a decree ordering a census of the whole world. Everyone went to register, each to his own town. And so Joseph went from the town of Nazareth in Galilee to Judea, to David's town of Bethlehem, because he was of the house and lineage of David, to register with Mary, his espoused wife, who was with child.
(Spotlight shines on Caesar in west balcony.)
Caesar: Fill out those census forms. *(Looks at people in audience near him in balcony.)* Why aren't they filled out already?
(House lights on.)
Caesar: *(leaning over railing on balcony and gesturing)* You children! Get up and collect those census forms! *(He walks down stairs shouting.)* I don't have time to waste! Be quick about it! *(Appearing in aisle at west door.)* You people are too slow! Pass those forms to the side aisles so the children can collect them!
(Caesar exits east door as lights dim.)
Narrator: While Joseph and Mary were there, the days of her confinement were completed. She gave birth to her first born son and wrapped him in swaddling clothes and laid him in a manger, because there was no room in the place where travelers lodged.
(Joseph and Mary enter north door walking down center aisle during this narration. When they are halfway down aisle, spotlight picks them up. They look to choir loft.) Any room up there?
Several Choir Members *(answer):* No room here.
Joseph and Mary: *(Turning to opposite loft.)* Any room up there?
Several Choir Members: No room here.
Joseph and Mary: *(looking directly at center ground floor audience)* Doesn't anyone have any room?
Audience: *(helped by Narrator)* No, we have no room.
(Joseph and Mary slowly exit east door as narrator continues.)
Narrator: Perhaps for one brief moment in Bethlehem time stood still while heaven kissed earth. The world that had waited so long for the Promise witnessed his coming in silence and welcomed him with disbelief. *(Lights dim.)* They expected a king and were given a child... a child that entered the stream of humanity and diverted its course... a child whose small arms became the bridge across the chasm of sin... a child whose life embraced the universe and became the still point of our turning world.
(Lights come up on stage as Adult choir begins to sing "Star Carol." Children's choir joins them on chorus as they build Manger Scene on stage. Individual children are assigned specific items to retrieve from behind right and left south stage doors — pillars, hay, manger. Still singing, children move downstage and form living border as Joseph and Mary enter south door stage right and position themselves on either side of manger. Beam of light focuses on center of manger symbolizing birth.)
Silent tableau one minute.

(Adult choir sings "Jazz Gloria" and all five dancers, each in different color pastel top, enter after first phrase forming a circle. At high point in song mirrored ball suspended from ceiling turns as house lights dim and flashes of light illuminate dancers and audience, then dancers exit as they entered.)

Narrator: Shepherds came and were never again the same. Wise men came and were never again the same. Prophets, priests, kings, and peoples came and were never again the same. Tonight we have come. Has he touched us? Can he make a difference? Will we ever be the same?

(Youth choir enters from stage right and left south doors carrying lighted candles, singing "I Wonder As I Wander." At completion of song they blow out candles and sit in front of stage. House lights on.)

Part III

(Adult Jesus enters from east door singing chorus of "Lord of the Dance." As he approaches stage, Youth choir speakers begin.)

Speaker I: Jesus, can I be with you wherever you go?

Speaker II: Yes, we want to be with you all the time.

Speaker III: Yeah, you're nice to us.

Jesus: You are all my brothers and sisters. Each of you may follow me forever, for it is my father's wish that you do so. *(Jesus seats himself on rock which Youth choir member has placed downstage left during above dialog.)* Come, my children, gather round and tell me what you feel.

Child I: Jesus, I love when we celebrate your birthday every year at Christmas.

Child II: But how come a lot of people were glad you were born and then hurt you so much and made you die?

Child III: Why did that have to happen, Jesus?

Jesus: People are still searching.

(Jesus moves among members of Children's and Youth choirs singing "Because God Loves You." At completion of song Jesus sits on first step of center stairs to sing "Lord of the Dance." While he is singing first verse, five dancers enter south door at stage right. First dancer carries large lighted candle and places it at Jesus' side, then moves to center stage with two dancers on either side and slightly forward and back of her to begin dancing at second verse. As final chorus is sung, dancers light individual small candles, passing them to Youth choir members, who in turn pass them to audience, who in turn light each other's candles. As a final unsung chorus of "Lord of the Dance" is played on harpsichord, Jesus, dancers, and Children's choir, march down center aisle shaking hands of audience and wishing them "Merry Christmas." While this is taking place, Adult choir has silently left choir loft and is taking position on stage in dimmed light. Guitar chords are heard from choir loft.)

102

Narrator: Prophets foretold it. Angels proclaimed it. The Lord fulfilled it. And we must live it! Hallelujah!
(Adult choir sings "Hallelujah Chorus." Upon completion of above, light dims while entire cast assembles in remaining space on stage and in front of stage and narrator continues.)
Narrator: A light shines in darkness to illuminate the nations! We invited you to "Come to the Stable... return to Bethlehem; "but now, we invite you to become Bethlehem, to make your heart his home. Join us as we sing "Silent Night." And remember, love was born in Bethlehem almost 2,000 years ago... and love is still the greatest power on earth! *(Audience joins in singing "Silent Night" and other favorite hymns.)*

Choreography

BABE OF BETHLEHEM

"Babe of Bethlehem" relies on interpretation of words, it begins with dancers (three) kneeling at oblique angle right of center stage.

Ye nations all,	Right arm makes half circle from heart to outside of body, palms up.
On ye I call,	Make same movement to left side.
Come hear this declaration,	Both arms circle inward chest level.
And don't refuse	Left arm straightens above head while left foot is placed flat on floor. (Weight is shifted to left foot at this time.)
This glorious news	Repeat arm and leg movements with right arm and right leg, shifting weight to right leg and standing.
Of Jesus and salvation.	Both arms circle out, down, and around, to end at waist.

To royal Jews	Step back right, touch left foot beside right.
Came first the news	Repeat to left while bringing both arms down to sides.
Of Christ, the great Messiah,	Step forward right, left, while bringing hands up to prayer position.
As was foretold by prophets old,	Lunge to right on right foot while extending right arm waist level in a half circle.
Isaiah, Jeremiah.	Step to up right on left, then on right , as right arm drops to side.

To Abraham the promise came *And to his seed forever.* *A light to shine in Isaac's line,* *By Scripture we discover;* *Hail promised morn the Savior's born,* *The glorious Mediator.* *God's blessed Word made flesh and blood,* *Assumed the human nature.*	Skip verses two and three.

His parents poor in earthly store,
To entertain the stranger,
They found no bed to lay his head,
But in the ox's manger;
No royal things as used by kings,
Were seen by those that found him.
But in the hay the stranger lay,
With swaddling bands around him.

On that same night	Step back right, touch left beside.
A glorious light	Repeat to left.

To shepherds there appeared,	Step forward right, left, as arms circle in, up, overhead, and out to shoulder level.
Bright angels came	Left foot steps back, right closes beside as right arm drops to side.
In shining flame,	Left foot steps back but right only touches beside left.
They saw and greatly feared,	Step forward right then bring both hands up toward side of face with palms out in fear gesture.
The angels said,	Step forward left as arms come straight down to sides.
"Be not afraid,"	Kneel on right knee as arms cross chest, palms resting on shoulders.
Although we much alarm you,	Tilt head to right while looking left.
We do appear	Stand up on left foot as left arm straightens.
Good news to bear,	Right foot steps back, left touches beside it.
As now we will inform you."	Left foot steps back, right touches beside, step forward right, left, as left arm drops to side, both palms facing forward.
Then with delight they took their flight, *And winged their way to glory,*	Step left brush right in front of left, left hop (modified), reverse, and repeat in order to travel to center of stage, arms relaxed at shoulder level.

The shepherds gazed and were amazed,	Step back left, right closes beside left, step back left, right touches beside left.
To hear the pleasing story;	Right steps forward, left touches beside as arms circle up and out at face level, palms out.
To Bethlehem they quickly came,	Repeat step brush hop left, right, as in first line.
The glorious news to carry,	Step in place left, right.
And in the stall they found them all, Joseph, the Babe and Mary.	Sway left, right, left, right.
The shepherds then returned Again to their own habitation,	Step right, left brushes in front of right, rise on ball of both feet and turn to right, step right on "again," step back left, close right, repeat with right foot touching beside left.
With joy of heart they did depart,	Step forward right, left, right, left.
Now they have found salvation;	Arms circle inward and upward to end shoulder level.
"Glory," they cry, "to God on high,	Left steps back, right closes beside left, repeat with right touching beside left, while left arm moves back and above head and right arm drops to side.
Who sent his son to save us!	Step forward right, left, as arms move out to shoulder level in crucifixion position.
This glorious morn a Savior's born,	Step back left, right close, repeat with right touching beside left.

His name is Christ Jesus."	Step forward right, left, then bring hands to prayer position.
The city's name is Bethlehem, In which God hath appointed,	Repeat step brush hop right, left, right, left, as explained in verse five, but move in circle to right.
This glorious morn a Savior's born, For him hath God anointed;	Repeat "glorious morn" step from above verse substituting arm half circle chest high (right arm) from left to right for crucifixion arms.
By this you'll know: If you will go, to see this little stranger,	Step brush hop step left, right, left, right in place.
His lovely charms in Mary's arms, Both lying in a manger.	Sway left, right, left, right.
When this was said, straightway was made	Step left, touch right beside, repeat to right.
A glorious sound from heaven:	Both arms circle in, up, and out to shoulder level.
Each flaming tongue an anthem sung,	Repeat "glorious morn" step.
"To men a Saviour's given,	Lunge right on right as right arm makes half circle across front of body and parallel with floor, palm up.
In Jesus' name,	Left foot crosses in front of right as right pulls up to releve while arms assume prayer position.
The glorious theme, we elevate our voices	Both feet flat on floor, releve on theme and hold for rest of phrase.

At Jesus' birth,	Step back left.
Be peace on earth,	Kneel down on right.
Meanwhile all heav'n rejoices."	Head up, both arms uplifted above head, palms inward.

"Christmas Concerto" should be done lightly, flowing in an almost un-earthly way. Each sentence of explanation requires two six counts. Move-ment begins from back, stage right, where Angel has been standing since entrance. Raise right arm in jazz port de bra (shoulder, elbow, wrist). Repeat with left arm. Lower both (shoulder, elbow, wrist). Cross arms in front of chest and open, with arms relaxed from shoulder while stepping forward left, right. Step toward center of stage left, right, while lowering arms to sides, palms out. Step forward left, cross right over left as right arm crosses body at chest, preparation. Right reverse turn. Walk forward right, left, right, left, arms opening to sides, chest level. Step forward left, kneel down right. Scoop both arms in at waist level, open to left, head tilted toward Mary. Rise from kneeling position while arms reach heavenward, almost straightening at elbows. Step closer to Mary left, right, left, right. Lay both hands on Mary's shoulders while Mary rises from kneeling position. Step back from Mary right, left, right, left as hands slowly pull away from her shoulders; Angel should feel as if she's a magnetic force pulling Mary.

This is the "mirroring" section where Mary and the Angel face each other, Mary's left side to audience, Angel's right side to audience. The count remains the same as in first part. Hand toward audience circles up, out, and around from waist level, as body leans into movement. Repeat to other side. Both hands up, front, over, and around to shoulder level. (Throughout these steps hands remain about six inches apart.) Angel steps back left, right as Mary steps forward right, left, each reaching for the other. Angel steps back again right, left, still reaching, as Mary re-mains in place, still reaching. Angel kneels on right knee with left foot on floor, left arm still extended to Mary who is still reaching for Angel. Both of Angel's arms lower to left knee, wrists crossed, and she freezes in this position while Mary dances.

"Mary's Dance" is done to two choruses of "Lord of the Dance" played slowly on piano. Each sentence requires eight counts. Turning toward front of stage, step right close left step right point left, reverse. Step right close left three times, point right twice while moving downstage right. Left hop right step left close, repeat; right points forward as arms scoop in chest level and fingertips meet. Step back right as both arms make parallel circle to left, over head, to right, and back to left. Repeat entire dance slightly more lively (music tempo increases slightly) substituting kneeling on right knee with left foot firmly on floor, arms and head raised heavenward, for parallel arm circles.

"Jazz Gloria" starts very subdued, builds, then peacefully fades off. Expressions on faces are important. Steps are named A through F to faciliate repeats. Count is 'one and.' Step A: dancers (five) move onto stage with this step, starting stage left, moving to right and around to form a circle facing inward. Arms at sides, step right close left eight times; on last step, left touches beside rather than closes. Step B (grapevine): left crosses over right, right steps side, left crosses behind right, right steps side. Do four times, on last right step to side merely touching right rather than stepping to facilitate repeating step to left. Repeat step to left, starting with right crossing over left, arms out and relaxed at shoulder level. Do step three times. On 'seven and eight and' do a three step turn right, left, right; touch left to outside, making circle larger. Repeat step A to left, ending with right foot touching beside left, then repeat same step to right, arms shoulder level. On final right step, left touch, turn body so that right side is on outside of circle. Step C: moving inward to make circle smaller and also to highlight mirrored ball which has been lowered from ceiling and has begun spinning, left arm angled overhead toward center, right arm angled down and to outside, step left, step right crossing over left, three times, step left, point right to outside, move right arm up to meet left and back down to side, repeat. Step D: left arm still angled overhead toward center, step right, touch left beside right; reverse; do eight times altogether. Repeat another eight times, substituting attitude kick for touch. Step E: cross and lift step, turn body to face outside of circle, cross right over left while bringing right arm across body to left, chest level, step left, lift right leg in attitude kick while raising right arm in arc above head to right side, shoulder level, step right to right side; reverse and repeat, turning in toward circle on final left step. Step F: walk with knees bent, in to make circle smaller, gradually raising arms above head, right, left, right, left. Step backward right, touch left beside, reverse and repeat; at last step left, touch right, turn body to face outside. Entire step requires one eight count. Repeat step B, grapevine, starting with right foot crossing over left, with arms shoulder level; repeat starting with left foot crossing over right, arms down at sides. Repeat step A, step close, to left, arms up shoulder level, unwinding circle and moving offstage.

LORD OF THE DANCE

I danced in the morning
When the world was begun,
And I danced in the moon,
And the stars and the sun,
And I came down from heaven
And I danced on the Earth
At Bethlehem I had my birth.

"Lord of the Dance" is an interpretation of words, with one dancer as Christ in center of stage, two dancers on either side at angle, dancers in front farther away from Christ than those in back. While stanza one is sung, dancers are moving into basic postions on stage, Christ dancer (carrying large lighted candle) moves to extreme front of stage just right of center, then places candle (in elaborate holder) on floor.

Refrain:
Dance then

Raise right knee while doing releve on left foot.
Drop to right knee, kneeling.

wherever you may be,

Rise to both feet and turn (Christ turns in place, scribes turn right, moving outward, fishermen turn left moving outward).

I am the Lord

Christ steps back left, raising arms above head in V.

of the Dance said He,
And I'll lead you all
Wherever you may be,
And I'll lead you all
In the dance said he.

Step forward right while lowering arms to chest level and keeping palms up. Other dancers do a three step turn, right, left, right, in place, raising opposite arm with each step, at the same time that Christ is dancing to the same phrase. For the remainder of the chorus all four dancers reach for Christ's hands, each walking toward Christ, then all drop hands to return to original positions.

I danced for the scribe
And the Pharisee
But they would not dance
And they wouldn't follow me.
I danced for the fishermen
For James and John.

Dancers at stage right pose as scribes; those at stage left pose as fishermen. Synchronous with words, Christ bows to scribes and then turns away as they turn away. Christ bows to fishermen who stretch out arms, each clasping

110

They came with me
And the dance went on.

one of his hands, then all bow. Christ returns to stage C for chorus.

Refrain

I danced on the Sabbath
And I cured the lame.
The holy people said
It was a shame.
They whipped and they stripped
And they hung me high
And they left me there
On a cross to die.

Stage right dancers pose as priests; left dancers pose as healthy person supporting lame person. Christ walks toward lame, reaches down and helps her stand. At the same time priests assume prayer hands and negatively shake heads. Priests then lift Christ's arms overhead while making whipping motions, leaving him in crucified position.

Refrain

Remains the same until "I lead you all," at which point all dancers take Christ's hands, move inward two steps, and bow.

I danced on a Friday
When the sky turned black.

Christ steps forward right, lowers left knee to floor, stretches arms and body over right knee and back in to hide face. At the same time, other dancers turn backs to Christ and side close step to form circular wall with arms stretched shoulder level behind him.

It's hard to dance
With the devil on your back.

Christ arches back touching wall as wall moves in to enclose him.

They buried my body
And they thought I'd gone.
But I am the dance
And I still go on.

Christ kneels on "buried," circle breaks at front center on "but I am the dance," then Christ leaps up while other dancers move to four corners of stage.

Refrain

Remains the same until "I will lead you all," when Christ points to each in turn and each turns toward him.

111

They cut me down
And I leapt up high.
I am the life
That'll never, never die.

Four corner dancers move to light in-dividual candles and pass them to Youth and Children's choir who then pass them to audience, while Christ dances last verse. Christ drops to knees from crucifixion position, leaps up, then steps forward right at the same time he is scooping arms down then up into prayer position then up into V.

I'll live in you

Right arm sweeps across chest

If you'll live in me
I am the Lord
Of the dance said He.

Same movement with left arm, then both arms open chest level, palms up.

Refrain

Repeat movements used in first chorus.

Virginia Shuker works with the dance in liturgy at the Catholic Church of St. Maurice in Fort Lauderdale, Florida. She has designed numerous dance dimen-sions in liturgies and has led workshops on using dance in worship. She is a member of the International Sacred Dance Guild and was a participant in the 1977 Sacred Dance Guild Institute.

11
Dancing Christmas Carols
With Youth Choirs

For junior high and high school youth who are beginning a dance choir or who have been together for a short time, these Christmas carol choreographies provide starting points. Have the dance choir try out these choreographies to evaluate which parts allow the youths genuine expression and which parts would need to be changed to allow such expression. The more developed the dance choir, the more they will create and recreate their own choreographies.

The moods of discouragement, entrapment, searching, beginning awareness, sensing new power, and strengthening community can be expressed in dramatic movement. The first three lines of each stanza are background for discouragement and searching; the fourth line of each stanza can be the bridge for dramatic action to express a growing awareness of possible release from despair. Then comes the rejoicing chorus where new power is experienced and a sense of God's presence is manifested in the gathered group.

O COME, O COME, EMMANUEL

O come, O come, Emmanuel,
And ransome captive Israel,
That mourns in lonely exile here

Any number of boys, girls, men and women slowly come down the aisles. They are crouching, bent with discouragement yet searching. They are wearing deep-colored jerseys, sweaters or shirts and may have long rectangular shawls of dark brown, purple and/or black. The girls and women may use the shawls to cover their heads but vary their movements by reaching in angles, stretching the shawl against the back of the head or across the top of the head. The boys or men can use their shawls as ropes or chains, stretching angularly against the body or winding the shawl like chains around the wrists in front or behind the back. The use of shawls often helps those who have not done much in dramatic dance to find a vehicle for strong movement. A variety of human misery is expressed during the first three lines.

Until the Son of God appear.

(Historical Chorus)
Rejoice! Rejoice! Emmanuel

On the fourth line (in the midst of crouched movements), each one starts to look up, face upturned, showing a ray of hope. Then on "Rejoice! Rejoice!" strong upward thrusts are made by all. A sense of rescue and release comes from the exhilerating reality of God's power. The shawls are left hanging around the neck during the first chorus; but on the last chorus, the shawls may be dropped or cast off on the floor.

Is come to thee,

O Israel.

On "Emmanuel is come to thee" or "Emmanuel is come to us," all dancers express their awareness that the remoteness is over, that they are here and now sensing God's power within and through them. Arms are not stretched upward, but come down centering as if receiving power. On "O Israel" or "And with us all does dwell," arms widen out as each one turns toward others, aware that God's presence is with everyone and draws us together. At the close, each one stands taller and straighter, shoulders, back, diaphragm lifted, head slightly raised, radiating the joy of "God with us."

O come now Dayspring, come and cheer
Our spirits by your advent here;
Disperse the gloomy clouds of night
And death's dark shadows put to flight.

(Contemporary Chorus)
Rejoice! Rejoice! Emmanuel
Is come to us and with us all does dwell!

114

Sometimes this interpretation can be enhanced if the church is in darkness except for a light in the chancel so that those coming down the aisles are dimly visible. When they reach the foot of the chancel, they are seen in silhouette and possibly with light coming down on them. A single voice in the back may sing the stanzas and a group of voices join in the chorus. In this way, the church may be kept in darkness.

To provide a response from the congregation, the lights may be increased so that the congregation can sing the second stanza and the chorus from a mimeographed service of worship. The dramatic dance group can go up the center aisle during the chorus, which they sing and express with upward reach and then outspread reaches toward the congregation.

If the congregation cares to join in some of the action of the chorus, the dramatic dance group should remain the chancel area and repeat the upward reach of the "rejoices," then lowering as receiving, then the reaching out toward others as a community. The congregation would be assured of what to do following the group in the chancel. After participating in the action for the chorus, the congregation can be asked or signaled to sit, bent over, with the words of the stanza in their laps or with the mimeographed sheet slipped into the hymn book rack and folded over so that the words can be read and sung with hands freed to move. Then all can stand to sing and express the chorus. In this way, all in the congregation have the opportunity to experience the moods of this ancient hymn of the Christian Church.

I WONDER AS I WANDER

This Appalachian carol has a simplicity and poignancy that fits in with Advent as well as with Christmas. Advent is that time when one wonders why Jesus came into the world to face death for the sake of ordinary ("or'nr'y") people like each one of us. The carol is meaningful at any time and especially when children and youth interpret it at a summer camp outdoors under the sky.

A group design for this carol has been worked out but should be adapted freely by your own group so their own creative ideas are incorporated to make it their own work. There is a background group of five, six, or seven who stand in a slightly curved arc upstage facing front. There is also one soloist in front of the group. This one stands at stage right, downstage.

Stanza One:
I wonder as I wander out under the
sky,

Group: Look up with faces uplifted; arms then rise gradually and slowly from the sides, palms of hands turned up. During "under the sky" the arms are extended high and wide, finger tips touching finger tips of the persons adjacent. Because the group is standing in a slight arc, peripheral vision should enable them to lift their arms at the same speed. But they should not look across at each other, for their gaze should be upward. Their peripheral vision can give them the clue.

Soloist: Lifting both arms forward chest level, then with left arm held forward, swing right arm up vertically, then backward so that both arms become held in a wide horizontal stretch at shoulder level. The soloist walks slowly to center of platform. The head is tipped backward, for the focus is upward.

How Jesus, our Savior,

Group: Slowly they lower their arms, drawing them in with palms facing each other. Focus is still high.

Soloist: Soloist draws arms toward chest, palms parallel but apart.

Did come to die

Group: Keeping the palms in the vertical position, the hands cross past each other at chest level. Everyone looks down.

Soloist: Soloist brings arms down twisting torso to the right. Hands become clenched and cross at the wrists and continue in a downward stretch. One knee is bent and the head is bowed.

For poor or'nr'y people

Group: Leaving left arm in place, move right arm down and to the right. Eyes follow the movement of the right hand.

Soloist: Leading with the left elbow

116

and with the palm turned down, rise and pivot to the left until around to front, but always following the leading left hand, so end looking left.

Like you and like I.

Group: Left arm moves down and to the left. Eyes follow movement of left hand.
Soloist: Repeat the pivoting design to the right.

I wonder as I wander

Group: Everyone looks up and the arms are raised slowly as in first line of this carol.
Soloist: Soloist moves around the front area, pausing at the end of "wander." Arms are extended horizontally as in the first line of the carol.

Out under the sky.

Group: Arms are upraised with no strain. Let the arms rest in the sockets at their shoulders which should be down.
Soloist: Continuing in the same wide armed spread and walking, comes to center, facing front, head and eyes upward.

Stanza Two:
When Mary birthed Jesus 'twas in a cow's stall,

Group: Everyone looks down at the soloist center. Arms are lowered slowly into peaked "praying hands" held at chest level.
Soloist: If soloist is female, she assumes the role of Mary, kneeling center, cradling an imagined child in her arms. If soloist is male, a center female of the background group comes forward and center to take the part of Mary, while the male soloist assumes the part of Joseph beside her.

With wisemen and farmers

Group: Two of background group (stage left) step forward and lean toward Mary.
Soloist (Mary): With her arms remaining "cradling," leans to the left as if showing her child to the wisemen and farmers.

And shepherds and all.

Group: Two of background group (stage right) step forward and lean toward Mary.
Soloist (Mary): Leans right to show her child to shepherds, etc.

But high from God's heaven

Group: The four who had stepped forward (two from each side) face toward each other with raised upstage arms, move toward each other and pass (like "right and left thru" in square dancing). They continue to the place where their opposite ones were standing, but they are facing off stage at this moment. Any others in background lift arms high.
Soloist: Mary lifts her head, looking upward. Or both Mary and Joseph look up.

A star's light did fall,

Group: The four (who have crossed past each other with upstage arms high and downstage arms extended downward diagonally) make a pivoting half turn and look center at soloist. The arms remain in the same position; since they have turned in, the diagonally down arm focuses on Mary, the arm that was up remains high at back. Any others in the original background group continue to hold arms uplifted.
Soloist: Mary bends down and seems to lay the child on the "hay." The cradled arms separate, almost touching the floor.

And the promise of ages	Group and Soloist: All in the entire group widen out into a circle and look up, lifting extended arms forward and on up to a high wide spread of arms on "ages."
It then did recall.	Group and Soloist: Remaining in the circle, all gradually lower arms outward and downward until spread at sides; focus is downward into the center of the circle.
Stanza Three: *If Jesus had wanted for any wee thing,*	Group and Soloist: All spread with spiral downward turns until each one kneels on one knee with right hand spreading close to the floor.
A star in the sky	Half of group at stage right cluster together with the tallest (with highest extension of left arm) as center person. Others mold into a closed group with single arms reaching vertically. Heads back, faces upturned. They hold this position during the next half of this line. Group at stage left has not moved.
Or a bird on the wing,	Half of the group at stage left rise, pivot and end with a forward diagonal lean toward stage right. The elbows are pulled back, heads lifted.
Or all of God's angels in heav'n for to sing,	Group and Soloist: All turn in place at least twice with arms vertically overhead waving slightly together and apart with wrists almost touching on the inward wave on "all," "an(gels)," "heav'n," "sing."
He surely could have had it	Group and Soloist: Everyone brings arms down forward with bent elbows leading. They turn toward upstage, as if toward an altar.

'Cause He was the King.

Everyone kneels on both knees, bends forward as arms slice down with backs of hands touching the floor. Then all lift heads and look up on "the King."

Stanza Four: (the same words as Stanza One)
I wonder as I wander out under the sky,

Group and Soloist: Everyone rises and walks into a circling design counter clockwise. Both arms outstretched are raised forward to shoulder level on "I wonder." Then with the left arm remaining in the forward position, the right arm swings upward, and backward until it is shoulder level, so arms are extended straight across forward and back. All look up.

How Jesus, our Savior,

Group and Soloist: Everyone draws arms together, crossing them at chest level on "Savior." Two steps forward in the large circle.

Did come to die

Group and Soloist: Everyone takes step forward, then bends the knees. All look down as arms crossed are lowered until they cross at the wrists, hands pointing downward, almost touching the floor. The body is turned out to the right.

For poor or'nr'y people

Group and Soloist: Rise and step forward on left; then leading with the right elbow and forearm, turn and make a complete pivot to the right. The focus is outward, a little above the extending right arm.

Like you and like I.

Group and Soloist: Step forward on right foot, then pivot to the left with left elbow and forearm leading and finally extending full length. The focus is outward, a little above the left hand.

120

I wonder as I wander

Group: Raising both arms wide, extended shoulder level, each one walks toward his/her original spot at the initial start of this carol (in the background line). On the second syllable of "wander," everyone turns, facing forward but looking up.
Soloist: With both arms raised wide and shoulder level, soloist moves down center, looking up.

Out under the sky.

Group: Everyone sustains the wide arm spread — no strain with a sense of acceptance and enjoyment of wonder. The arms should "rest" in the shoulder sockets; and the shoulders should be straight and resting down with no strain. The head is tipped backward, mouth may be slightly open, eyes looking straight up. This position is held until the end of the music, then slowly lowered. Then all leave the chancel.
Soloist: Soloist continues across to the farthest edge of stage left, and holds the position until the end of the music, then lowers arms and leaves.

ALL PRAISE TO THEE (Tallis Canon)
(Four Part Round)

This Christmas hymn was written by Martin Luther. The music is the familiar Tallis Canon in most hymnals with the first line "All praise to thee, my God, this night." For the purpose of the design in the sequence form of a round, we use just the first stanza of Luther's hymn.

Although this canon is to be sung in eight parts, the dance pattern as a round is in four parts, with a definite design for each line. Then the harmony is achieved as each line is started successively. First of all, let each group of four abreast learn the full design for all four lines of the hymn. There will be four groups moving, but each group must learn the one pattern. In the graph design, one group will be OOOO, another VVVV, another XXXX, and the last ZZZZ. The simple design will be illustrated alone with OOOO.

Encourage inter-generational activities through this and other carols. The messages of "Glory to God" and "Goodwill toward all" can be experienced through joining together in symbolic dance. This canon (round) has been danced by boys and girls (10 years and older) and men and women (even 80 years old). One man was 82 years old when he danced in this. If some cannot kneel and rise easily, then in the one place kneeling is suggested, substitute a genuflection.

All praise to thee Eternal Lord (8 counts)

All advance eight steps toward altar. All raise both arms with full stretch upward, head back on "Lord."

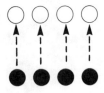

Clothed in a garb of flesh and blood (8 counts)

All lower arms and the two on the left turn left and the two on the right turn right and walk downstage along the outside edges. Arms are slightly extended, eyes down.

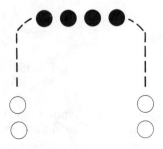

Choosing a manger for thy throne (8 counts)

All turn toward center, take three steps into center, then kneel as a group of four together. All looking down.

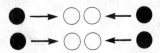

While worlds on worlds are thine alone (8 counts)

All rise, look up and thrust arms straight up. Those on the right turn right downstage, then continue to turn around slowly to the right, but edge out a little from the center. When they have turned until they face the altar, hold arms high, with head back thru the singing of "alone."

Those on stage left follow the same design except that they make their turn to the left. All are now facing the altar so that they are ready to merge closer together, going forward to repeat the first line of this stanza and continue the same design.

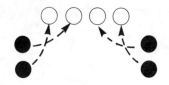

When each of the four units has learned this simple design, then start the merging in round form, but start merging with just the Os and Vs first. Have them go through the sequence twice. The Vs will be singing and moving to the successive line that the Os just finished.

Then merge in the three parts, having the Xs interrelate with the Os and Vs. Then merge the Zs into the design. They must all learn to stay in the proper areas or a "traffic jam" will occur. They will learn this quickly if each group is merged in step by step.

The diagrams show the relative positions of each group at the close (eighth count) of each line through the first stanza. Then the repeat stanza dove-tails without a break. (It is just like singing "Three Blind Mice" twice through.)

Pattern as a round
(up stage) (altar)
(stage right) (stage left)
            (downstage)

Starting position:

O O O O
V V V V
X X X X
Z Z Z Z

End of line 1 for O

O O O O

V V V V
X X X X
Z Z Z Z

End of
line 2 for O
line 1 for V

V V V V

X X X X
Z Z Z Z
O   **O**
O   **O**

End of
line 3 for O
line 2 for V
line 1 for X

X X X X

Z Z Z Z

V   OO   V
V   OO   V

End of
line 4 for O
line 3 for V
line 2 for X
line 1 for Z

Z Z Z Z

** O   O**
X O V V O X
X   V V   X

*Continue on through a second time
and end with "Amens."*

How do we end? We find this effective: After the Os have completed the repeat of the stanza and they are facing the altar, they sing "Amen" four times for the first line as they go up close to the altar with arms raised high singing "Amens" throughout the rest of the stanza; but they bring their arms down at the close of the last two "Amens."

Similarly with the Vs and the Xs as they complete the repeated stanza, they proceed toward the altar standing directly behind the Os. Arms are raised and they sing "Amens." But they lower their arms when the Os do, at the close of their stanza of "Amens." The Vs and Xs stop singing then even though they have not completed the singing of their respective stanzas.

When the Zs have completed their repeated stanza and turned toward the altar, they have just one line to move in behind the Xs, and this is the line when the Zs must be ready to lower their arms very soon after they get in the line behind the Xs.

As all arms are lowered, the hands can be brought into a "prayer position." All singing stops. With heads unbowed, all stand still for four counts before leaving the chancel.

The interweaving of the four parts of this round can be enhanced by accenting each group with a different color (possibly red, green, gold, and purple). There can be collars as in singing choirs, or gauntlet cuffs or tubular sleeves slipped up to fasten at the shoulder, or tunics. The use of four colors accentuates the constant changing of the design sequence, forming a kaleidoscope effect.

The choreography suggested can be adapted for use with two persons in each of the four parts or even six in each part. It can be presented with just three parts instead of four by eliminating the Zs. Also, this design can be adapted for the last stanza of the Tallis Canon found in most hymnals (first line: "All praise to thee, my God, this night.") The last stanza is the Doxology words that all know. The only change needed is a reversal of lines three and four. During line three ("Praise Him above ye heavenly host") have arms high as they turn and end facing the center. During line four ("Praise Father, Son, and Holy Ghost") cluster center and kneel. This is round for all seasons.

The congregation can be divided to sing the four parts of this canon. When they do it well, they feel a part of the dancers. It is important to have four leaders that will help them start and stay with them to the end.

GOOD CHRISTIAN FOLK REJOICE

This folk carol is done in two concentric circles. The inner circle is usually composed of the tallest persons. Each one in the inner circle continously holds a wreath in his or her right hand. Each may touch the wreath of the person to the left, but never takes it from the neighbor.

The outer circle is made up of shorter persons. Each one holds red/green cords (about 1 ½ yards long) with knotted ends held in each hand. These may be green garlands, perhsps with bells on the ends of both garlands and wreaths.

126

Good Christian folk rejoice	All in inner circle, with wreath in right hand and touching wreath of person at left, step to the right with the tripudium step: right, left, right, and rest back on left. All in outer circle hold their cords outstretched with hands touching the hands of adjacent ones. Hands are held shoulder high. They use the tripudium to the right and on the third step they accent the "rejoice" by reaching farther to the right and then balance back on the left foot.
With heart and soul and voice.	Both circles continue with the same pattern.
Give ye heed to what we say,	All in inner circle step on right foot, turning to face outward and step on left. Holding the wreath in right hand close to chest while turning out, then sweep the wreath out toward "people" and continue with wide sweep ending to the right (as if spreading the "good news"). All in outer circle step on right foot, turning to face outward, then on the left foot and kneel. Hold the cords with hands close to chest during the right turn, then bring the hands outstretched and extended toward "people."
Jesus Christ is born today.	Now both circles are facing outward and both circles move to the left with wreaths and cords held as in line 1. Use tripudium: left, right, left and rest back on right.
Ox and ass	All in inner circle turn left toward center and hold wreaths close to chest while turning. All in outer circle turn left toward center and hold ends of cord close to chest.

before him bow,	All in both circles kneel and bring wreaths/cords forward.
And he is in the manger now.	All bow heads on "And he is in." Then all raise heads on "manger now."
Christ is born today,	All in inner circle rise and step toward center with right foot. All reach inward and high with wreaths so that they touch. All in outer circle rise and step center with right foot and reach diagonally toward center with right hand high and cord stretched right.
Christ	All smile throughout this line. Accent this by a further upward stretch by all.
is born	All face outward, shift weight to left foot while drawing wreath/cords close to chest.
today.	Those in inner circle step out with right foot and swing wreaths toward "people." Those in outer circle step outward on right foot, lean forward with slightly bent right knee. Arms are extended toward the "people."
Good Christian folk rejoice	Same as line 1 in Stanza 1
With heart and soul and voice.	Same as line 2 in Stanza 1
Now you hear of endless bliss,	Same as line 3 in Stanza 1

128

Jesus Christ was born for this.	Same as line 4 in Stanza 1
He has op'ed	Both circles turn left into center and kneel. They look upward. Inner circle holds wreaths high.
the heav'nly door	All in inner circle lean back, extend and widen arms.
And all are blessed	All lean forward and bow heads. Arms are lowered part way.
forevermore.	All lift heads and look up
Christ is born for this	Same as in line 7 in Stanza 1
Christ is born for this	Same as in line 8 in Stanza 1

This is a joyous carol and everyone should feel at home with the dance pattern so that everyone can smile freely during both stanzas except for lines 5 and 6 in each stanza. They are rejoicing and sharing the good news for all around them. This is effective when the observers are sitting "in the round" and the dancers can smile directly into the eyes of the observers and reach toward them.

If you have extra wreaths and cords, you will find that many of the observers will be glad to form a circle around the wreath circlers; and others will form a circle around the cord circlers. Then they can quickly learn either part in this way. What joy to be welcomed into participation!

Margaret Taylor is the author of numerous books on the history and contemporary practice of dance in worship. She has led dance in worship in over 400 churches in this country and abroad. Having served as International president of the Sacred Dance Guild, she was recently honored by the establishment of the "Margaret Taylor Endowment for Dance in Worship and Education" at Pacific School of Religion, Berkeley. Her books most related to Christmas Carol Dancing include: *A Time To Dance: Symbolic Movement In Worship* and recently *Dramatic Dance With Children In Worship and Education.* She continues to lead workshops across the country as she travels from her home in Oberlin, Ohio.

bibliography

STANDARD WORKS ON CHRISTMAS CAROLS

Dearmer, Percy; Williams, Vaughan R.; and Shaw, Martin, *The Oxford Book of Carols*, London: Oxford University Press, 1964.
As the classic collection of carols with music, this volume was first published in 1928. Although some of the carols are given in French, German, and Italian as well as in English translation, most are given only in English. Included are carols from Easter as well as Christmas and other church seasons. Some modern carols are included.

Greene, Richard Leighton, *The Early English Carols*, Oxford: Clarendon Press, 1935.
In this definitive work on carol lyrics, the carols are arranged by subject. This volume gives extensive treatment to the dance forms of carols, with one chapter devoted to these forms and providing detailed descriptions of some historic steps and patterns.

Stevens, J. E., *Medieval Carols* (Volume 4 of *Musica Britannica*), London: Stainer and Bell, 1952.
In this definitive work on carol scores, there are 135 musical settings given. These are late settings, as early scores have not survived.

POPULAR WORKS ON CHRISTMAS CAROLS

Duncan, Edmonstoune, *The Story of the Carol*, New York: Charles Scribner's Sons, 1911.
If historically inaccurate in many places, this volume has the virtue of imagination in tracing the carol form to similar forms in Greek culture. Because solid historical tracing of the carol roots is probably impossible, this volume's approach is suggestive, but not conclusive.

Routley, Erik, *The English Carol*, London: Herbert Jenkins, 1958.
Although not an original scholarly work, this volume is a popular treatment and reliable on the use of the carols in worship. Carol services are suggested for contemporary worship, even though the author is concerned primarily with carols as music, not dance.

Langstaff, John, M.; *The Season for Singing, American Christmas Songs and Carols*; New York: Doubleday and Company, Inc., 1974.

Simon, Henry, W., *A Treasury of Christmas Songs and Carols*, Boston: Houghton Mifflin Company, 1955.

Walter, L. Edna, *Christmas Carols, Old English Carols for Christmas and other Festivals*, New York: The Macmillan Company, 1922.

Wheeler, Opal, *Sing for Christmas*, New York: E. P. Dutton and Company, Inc., 1958.

WORKS ON DANCING CHRISTMAS CAROLS

Adams, Doug, *Congregational Dancing in Christian Worship*, Austin: Sharing Company, 1977.
Exploring early church as well as later forms of dance in Christian worship, this volume develops the theological and biblical guidelines as well as many dance forms for folk dancing in contemporary worship.

Adams, Doug, *Involving The People In Dancing Worship: Historic and Contemporary Patterns*, Grand Rapids: Sacred Dance Guild, 1975.
Among the dance forms of other periods that might be utilized in contemporary worship, the tripudium is fully described in its functions as the people's movement during the chorus of Christmas carols.

Backman, E. Louis, *Religious Dances In The Christian Church*, London: Allen and Unwin Ltd. 1952.
Backman spent a lifetime translating the passages related to dance in the works of Greek and Latin church fathers. Although not theologically or biblically trained, Backman has provided the basic texts and translations. He did not, however, understand the significance of much of the material.

DeSola, Carla, *The Spirit Moves: A Handbook for Dance In Prayer*, Washington DC: The Liturgical Conference, 1977.
DeSola provides a section of this book with a few of the Christmas carols she has developed for the Mass; but most of the dancing carols are a part of her street caroling in New York at Christmas and are suggestive for other groups to spread the Christmas message not only by song but also by dance through any city.

Taylor, Margaret, *A Time To Dance: Symbolic Movement In Worship*, Austin: The Sharing Company, 1976.
Not only does Taylor provide description of historic and contemporary patterns of carol dancing, but her volume is greatly enriched by many photographs of art works (paintings from churches and museums) that show patterns of the dances.

Taylor, Margaret, *Dramatic Dance With Children In Worship and Education*, Austin: The Sharing Company, 1977
With choreographies creatively designed for the skills of children five through eleven (there are separate sections for each age group), this volume will be most helpful to teachers and worship leaders who work with pre-adolescents. But many of the dance patterns may be adapted for older youth and adults, especially for inter-generational worship.

Index of Carols Danced in this Book

Other Titles from RESOURCE

Advent and Christmas

Make Ready The Way *by Jean Evans*
A journal book for advent. **$3.95**
Family ADVENTures *by Bruce Clanton, SDS*
A family activity for each day of advent **$3.95**
Winter Dreams *by Joe Juknialis*
Christmas stories and other stories **$6.95**

Lent and Holy Week

The Holy Week Book *edited by Eileen Freeman*
A complete treatment of Holy Week Liturgy **$19.95**

Other Dance Resources

Dancing With Creation *by Martha Ann Kirk*
Choreographies and spirituality through twelve Native
American and Mexican American folk dances **$6.95**
Actions, Gestures, and Bodily Attitudes *by Carolyn Deitering*
A classic look at the basic movements, showing how and
why they can be spiritually uplifting. **$9.95**

Available at your local
dealer in creative resources for worship.